THE BASEBALL ANTHOLOGY

125 Years of Stories, Poems, Articles, Photographs, Drawings,
Interviews, Cartoons, and Other Memorabilia

The Cleveland Spiders of the 1890s: First competitive, then infamous, and now just another colorful chapter in baseball's 125-year history.

Overleaf left: "Iron Man" Joe McGinnity pitched for the New York Giants during the famously bizarre 1908 pennant race.

Overleaf right: After the Giants' Fred Snodgrass made a crucial error in the 1912 Series, The New York Times lamented: "Write in the pages of world's series baseball history the name of Snodgrass. Write it large and black."

Second overleaf: The World Champion 1915 Boston Red Sox. Note the cheerful rookie standing just right of center in the third row: Babe Ruth.

Rogers Hornsby, whose lifetime .358 batting average
ranks second in major league history.

Overleaf: Phil Rizzuto (sliding), scrappy shortstop for the
Yankee dynasty during the forties and fifties.

Baltimore's brilliant Brooks Robinson seemed to take every unreachable ball as a personal insult.

Overleaf: Steve Garvey, who always saved his most scintillating play for when it counted.

Second overleaf: The incomparable Ozzie Smith, premier shortstop of the 1980s and '90s.

Dave Winfield, who has played with unquenchable intensity for more than twenty years.

Opposite: The Colorado Rockies' Andres Galarraga, 1993 National League batting champion.

THE BASEBALL ANTHOLOGY

125 Years of Stories, Poems, Articles, Photographs, Drawings, Interviews, Cartoons, and Other Memorabilia

GENERAL EDITOR: JOSEPH WALLACE

FOREWORD BY SPARKY ANDERSON

HARRY N. ABRAMS, INC., PUBLISHERS

AN OFFICIAL PUBLICATION OF MAJOR LEAGUE BASEBALL

Editor: Sharon AvRutick
Design: Eric Baker Design Associates, Inc.
    with Patrick Seymour
Photo Editor: John K. Crowley
Text Permissions: Lauren Boucher

Library of Congress Cataloging-in-Publication Data

The Baseball anthology : 125 years of stories, poems, articles, photographs, drawings, interviews, cartoons,
and other memorabilia / general editor, Joseph Wallace.
    p. cm.
Consists of excerpts from books and articles from newspapers and magazines originally published 1868–1993.
Includes index.
ISBN 0-8109-3135-4
1. Baseball—United States—History.   I. Wallace, Joseph E.
GV863. A1B3765 1994
796.357'0973—dc20   94–5499

Printed and bound in Japan

Pittsburgh's Forbes Field, 1909.

DEDICATION
In memory of my father, who
in 1964 bought me a green
plastic Sinclair dinosaur at the
New York World's Fair and then
took me to Shea Stadium to see
my first baseball game.

WHO'S WHO IN BASEBALL

Price
25c

TWENTY-
THIRD
EDITION

Complete Life Records of More Than
220 Major League Ball Players

JOE
MEDWICK
1938

CONTENTS

25

PART THREE 1921–1945: THE GAME IN ITS GLORY

PAGE 184

PART FOUR 1946–1975: YEARS OF PEACE

PAGE 236   PART FIVE 1976–1994: FACING THE FUTURE

FOREWORD

By Sparky Anderson
Manager, Detroit Tigers

If you want to know about baseball, just take a look at the kids. If you want to know what it means to all of us, just ask the kids.

I'm not talking about just the kids in high school and college. I'm talking about those kids who play the game in the sandlots and parks in every city around the country.

As little kids, we make our first steps into the world of baseball with our parents' help. Then, when we become parents, we take our kids to games, and later they wind up taking their own kids, down the line. That's the beauty of baseball. It has a way of stringing families and generations together, making memories that are treasured for a lifetime.

Just as the love of baseball is passed down from generation to generation, so stories of players from the past are shared as well. In this 125th year of professional baseball, it seems right to reflect on the love of the game and its players—past, present, and future. Baseball and the tales of its heroes are so much a part of us that I can't imagine American life without them.

In a lifetime as a fan, I got the chance to watch stars like Ted Williams, Stan Musial, Willie Mays, Mickey Mantle, Bob Feller, and dozens of others. And in almost twenty-five years as a manager in Cincinnati and Detroit I've had the good fortune to actually get to know some of baseball's greatest legends. I managed Johnny Bench, Joe Morgan, Tom Seaver, Kirk Gibson, Jack Morris, Lou Whitaker, and other stars on magnificent teams that won seven division championships, five pennants, and three World Series.

But there's so much that I've missed, and that's why I turn to a book like this one with such pleasure. It gives me the opportunity to spend time with old heroes and modern legends; it puts me in touch with that essential part of me that's spelled baseball.

Those of us lucky enough to be part of the game have a tremendous responsibility—we're charged with giving back to the game all the good things the game has given us. Through our actions and words, and with books such as this one, we share baseball's great past with the generation of future stars, and their kids, and so on for at least another 125 years.

Before the Yankees became the Yankees and occupied
the House that Ruth Built, they called themselves the
Highlanders and played here, in Manhattan's Hilltop Park.

Overleaf: The Babe, in a posture he assumed 714 times.

PREFACE

"My main job, as I conceived it, was to continue to try to give the feel of things—to explain the baseball as it happened to me, at a distance and in retrospect. And this was the real luck, for how could I have guessed then that baseball, of all team sports anywhere, should turn out to be so complex, so rich and various in structure and aesthetics and emotion, as to convince me, after ten years as a writer and forty years as a fan, that I have not yet come close to its heart?"

Roger Angell, *The Summer Game* (1972)

No game has exerted a more powerful or enduring grip on writers than baseball. Every incident, every change, in the 125-year history of the professional game has been observed and reported in minute detail, leaving a priceless record of the growth of both the young game and the maturing country that embraced it.

I've been a baseball fan for more than thirty years, but thanks to the efforts of baseball writers my memories of the game extend back far before I was born. I never saw Ty Cobb play, or Babe Ruth, or Ted Williams, but I've gotten to know them all through the eyes of those writers lucky enough to have been there and skilled enough to communicate their excitement and pleasure.

In *The Baseball Anthology,* I trace the game's history through a selection of some of the finest baseball writing I found in reviewing hundreds of sources. Most of the ninety-seven excerpts have never been reprinted since their original publication, and a few are being published here for the first time. All provide a fresh, immediate perspective on baseball's colorful and varied past, as well as the entertaining characters who have populated the game.

The selections included here come from a wide range of sources: The wonderful, unjustly neglected *Spalding,*

Reach, and other annual baseball guides, written with both passion and precision by Francis Richter, Henry Chadwick, John Buckingham Foster, and other brilliant early supporters of the game; original newspaper accounts that gloried in the responsibility of providing all the color later assumed by radio and television; autobiographies of stars from Mike Kelly to Cap Anson to Mickey Cochrane to Hank Aaron; and such periodicals as *Baseball Magazine, Baseball Digest, Sports Illustrated,* and *Sport.*

Many of the most famous writers on baseball are included, of course—but I've intentionally focused on lesser-known gems, many long out of print, by Grantland Rice, Red Smith, Jim Murray, Roger Kahn, Roger Angell, and Thomas Boswell. In fact, you won't see excerpts from such classics as *The Boys of Summer* or *The Glory of Their Times*—not because they don't deserve inclusion, but because they are readily available in bookstores and libraries, while most of the pieces chosen are not.

The plethora of fine baseball history books in recent years has made many of the crucial events of the game's past—the Black Sox scandal, Jackie Robinson breaking down the color barrier—almost as familiar to today's fans as to those who lived through them. Rather than relying on such works as *Eight Men Out* and *Only the Ball Was White,* or the historical analyses produced by the Society for American Baseball Research, I've chosen to deconstruct these histories, going back to earlier, contemporary sources. So the events of 1919 are described by Hugh Fullerton (the writer who blew the whistle on the Black Sox), the editors of the *Reach Guide* and *Baseball Magazine,* and Buck Weaver; and the controversy surrounding Jackie Robinson's 1947 arrival in the big leagues is vividly recounted by participants Branch Rickey, Leo Durocher, and Robinson himself.

To sketch in a past that couldn't be fairly covered in ninety-seven excerpts, I've written a short historical introduction to each of the book's five sections. The responsibility for any errors or omissions in these essays—or in the selection of excerpts—is entirely my own.

Then again, some of the omissions may be intentional. Have I slighted your favorite team? Ignored a prized player? Slandered an entire era that you think was the best ever? Let me know, and we can have something to argue about during those long winter weeks until pitchers and catchers report.

I owe a debt of gratitude to many individuals who helped me put this book together. The library and copy service staff of the New York Public Library taught me to navigate the massive and essential Spalding Collection of baseball books, photographs, and memorabilia; Tom Heitz and Bill Deane at the National Baseball Hall of Fame Library took time out from a harried move to new quarters to show me their treasures, many of which made it into this book; Michael Bernstein, Cynthia McManus, Dana Nicole Williams, and Jennifer Langness at Major League Baseball Properties opened doors that otherwise would have remained closed; Stephanie Kelly of the Baltimore Orioles, Deb Madsen of the Boston Red Sox, Greg Schwallenberg of the Babe Ruth Museum, and Dick Johnson of the New England Sports Museum let me sift through their archives; and Mark Rucker of Transcendental Graphics bailed us out time and again.

Thanks also to Paul Gottlieb, publisher and editor-in-chief of Abrams; Sharon AvRutick (editor); John Crowley (picture editor); Lauren Boucher (text permissions); and Eric Baker, Patrick Seymour, and Rymn Massand (designers), who all did inspired work on insanely tight schedules.

*Sunshine, green grass, the game underway. As Ernie
Banks said: "Let's play two!"*

Overleaf: Lou Gehrig, the Iron Horse.

PART ONE

1869–1900:

A GAME TAKES HOLD

Abner Doubleday, known as the inventor of baseball, despite undeniable evidence to the contrary.

By 1869, the first year of truly professional baseball in the United States, the game was already an American passion. Even the tiniest village fielded its own team, and larger towns organized leagues. Local rivalries, as fierce as any seen today, sprang up. No one planned this love affair between mid-1800s America and the game; no one created or even foresaw it. Only later did entrepreneurs begin to understand baseball's great money-making potential.

Many guardians of baseball's privileged position as America's national pastime have claimed that the game was invented by Abner Doubleday in Cooperstown, New York, in 1839. It's a nice story, but it simply isn't true. Primitive versions of the sport—some even called base-ball—were known for decades before the date of Doubleday's "invention."

By insisting on an American birth for baseball, early writers sought to deny an embarrassing truth: That baseball actually was a direct descendant of rounders, a game most often played by British schoolchildren, which also involved a pitcher, a batter (called a "striker"), and four "bases," stones or posts placed in a diamond-shaped pattern. Any hint of British birth was anathema to an ex-colony with vivid memories of the all-too-recent Revolutionary War—so most writers and fans simply ignored the facts. Ex-player, writer, and sporting-goods magnate Albert Spalding's early-1900s comment was typical: "I have been fed on this kind of 'Rounder pap' for upward of forty years," he said, "and I refuse to swallow any more of it."

Despite its unfortunate parentage, American versions of the British schoolyard game soon began to spread across the country. No organized rules existed: Early variations called town-ball and round-ball might include twenty men on a

BOY'S BOOK OF SPORTS.   9

GAMES AT BALL.

The ball is a favorite toy, not only with those for whom
our little book is designed, but often with 'children of a
larger growth.' The number of different games played
with it is very great, but the limits of our book will only
allow us to describe some of the most common.
'Base ball' is played by a number, who are divided into
two parties, by the leader in each choosing one from
among the players alternately. The leaders then toss up

side, but all still revolved around bat, ball, and bases. "The ball games of the period were admirably suited to a young, essentially rural America," pointed out Harold Seymour in *Baseball: The Early Years* (1960), his classic history of the game. "Playing sites were plentiful and convenient. . . . Equipment was cheap and easy to come by."

The first known organized baseball team, the Knickerbocker Base Ball Club of New York, came into existence in 1845 at the suggestion of Alexander Cartwright, an employee of the New York Fire Department. The club, limited to forty members, played baseball games at Elysian Fields in Hoboken, New Jersey. Although the game differed greatly from the one we watch today, certain immutable rules had already been established, such as nine men to the side, ninety-foot basepaths, and three outs in each half inning.

The Knickerbocker Club's games must have attracted attention, for by the late 1850s the Knickerbockers had been joined by many other clubs in the New York area, as well as in New England, the Midwest, and even California. Interest in baseball was booming among spectators as well, with hundreds overflowing rickety, makeshift grandstands to cheer their teams on.

Top: Children playing rounders, 1832.
Above: A game of four o'cat, an early American precursor of baseball.

By the time the Civil War began, more than fifty clubs had joined baseball's first governing organization: The National Association of Base Ball Players, whose goals included establishing uniform rules and regulations for the game. Even during the war, the game and the Association retained much of their popularity, further testament to baseball's hold on the nation's imagination.

Baseball flourished as never before after the conflict ended. In the late 1860s, the number of spectators at important games might top ten thousand, and each year saw the appearance of new teams and new rivalries. Newspapers and magazines reported scores, and annual guidebooks such as *Beadle's Dime Base Ball Player* and the *De Witt Base-Ball Guide* listed rules changes, described exciting games, and detailed the organization of new leagues across the country.

Throughout this period of explosive growth, baseball was still supposed to be an amateur sport. Official rulebooks, in fact, often contained regulations specifically prohibiting the paying of players. Violators were threatened with forfeiture of games and other punishments, including expulsion from the National Association.

But no game so popular could remain amateur for long. While the Knickerbockers and other early clubs, whose members were wealthy to begin with, had considered baseball an enjoyable pastime to be played socially (à la cricket in England), by the late 1860s the game was played by men who saw it as a way to earn a livelihood. Moreover, communities could not fail to see the potential for profit in such a wildly popular diversion—or notice that profits would be greater if the teams were better, no matter how their players were obtained. The paying of players was so common by 1868 that the *De Witt Guide,* for one, despaired of trying to reform the corrupt existing teams, instead calling upon newly formed clubs "to taboo those who make a business of the game."

Top: The Knickerbockers and Excelsiors (1858): Two teams that could claim to have played baseball "when it was a game."

Above: Organized games had begun to draw large crowds by the 1860s.

This hope must have seemed forlorn even to the guide's editors, but it became sheerest fantasy in 1869, when a group of enterprising civic leaders turned to a famous player named Harry Wright and gave him license to prove once and for all that baseball had become a lucrative professional sport—planting the seed of the game that reached 125 years of age in 1994.

Wright's mission was to put together the best possible team that money could buy. Paying $1400 to his brother George, a brilliant shortstop, $1200 to himself, $1100 to pitcher Asa Brainard, and lesser amounts to ten other players, Harry Wright built the Cincinnati Red Stockings, a team that toured the country in 1869, overwhelming local teams wherever they played. Cincinnati finished the tour with something close to sixty wins (the exact number is controversial) and not a single loss.

Despite their impressive salaries, Harry Wright and the Red Stockings weren't treated like kings at every stop during their travels. In a journal he kept on the 1869 tour, Wright described a game delayed by inclement conditions. "Rained very heavy for about 20 Minutes, flooding the ground," he wrote. "We got some brooms, swept the water off, and put sawdust on the muddy places, and commenced playing."

Of course, the baseball played by the Red Stockings and their hapless opponents differed greatly from today's game; as baseball historian Bill James points out in his *Historical Baseball Abstract* (1985), baseball at the time resembled fast-pitch softball more than anything else—but it didn't resemble any modern game very closely. The pitcher was required to throw underhand, but he was also expected to place the pitch where the batter requested it. When the batter then whacked the ball, the fielders were forced to catch it barehanded. Not surprisingly, there were countless fielding errors, resulting in scores that seem embarrassingly high from a modern perspective. Teams might score sixty, eighty, even 100 runs a game. (The Blue Jays–Phillies 15–14 slugfest in the 1993 World Series would have counted as a pitcher's duel.)

The Cincinnati Red Stockings finally lost a game during their 1870 tour. Worse, the team itself went out of business at the end of that season, although the Wrights and other players soon turned up on other teams. By then the Red Stockings' legacy was clear.

Just a year later, in 1871, the first professional baseball organization, the National Association of Professional Base Ball Players, was formed. This loosely knit league struggled along until 1875, suffering from a lack of centralized leadership and no agreement on ticket prices, among other handicaps. Contemporary accounts make it clear that widespread gambling, the throwing of games (called "hippodroming"), and the jumping of star players from team to team ("revolving") also contributed to the National Association's end.

Despairing of solving these problems within the disorganized structure of the National Association, William A. Hulbert, a Chicago businessman and officer of the Chicago Base Ball Club, took his and three other teams out of the Association, forming the National League of Professional Baseball Clubs in 1876. In doing so, they took a giant step toward establishing the team owners' authority over the game and its players. A president and other officials were hired to enforce the rules and to establish some degree of uniformity throughout the League, and organized baseball began to assume a structure similar to that seen today.

Not to say that the National League was granted smooth sailing throughout its early years. Some of the other professional leagues that were springing up throughout the country featured baseball of scarcely lower quality and rivaled

the N.L. in popularity and financial stability. Throughout the 1880s and
'90s, the *Spalding Guide* and *The Sporting News* would devote a large
amount of space to the workings of the Eastern, Pacific Coast,
International, and other leagues—which at the time boasted independent
teams, not farm teams for the major league.

    The N.L. owners accepted the presence of these leagues, which in
general stayed away from N.L. sites. The owners were less sanguine,
though, about the occasional attempt by ambitious entrepreneurs to
establish new leagues in direct competition with the older league. At least
one of these competitors, the American Association (1882–91), at times
actually outstripped the National League in popularity. By locating its
teams in large cities (such as New York and Philadelphia) unaccountably
left out of the National League, charging lower admission, and selling beer
at games, the Association soon gained enough power to force an
agreement with the older league. This peace led to the playing of a
handful of championship series, casual affairs that frequently resembled
modern exhibition games.

    Despite the inroads made by the American Association and other
new leagues, the National League produced the first generation of true
baseball superstars. Today, only a few of these are widely remembered.
Among them are Mike "King" Kelly, whose devilish mind (he is said to

*The Detroit Wolverines, led by Hall of Famers
Dan Brouthers (left) and Sam Thompson,
topped the National League in 1887.*

have once inserted himself into a game just
in time to catch a foul pop near the dugout)
kept League magnates changing the rules to contain him; Willie Keeler, who "hit 'em where
they ain't"; Cap Anson; and John McGraw, perhaps better known for his presence in the
game after the turn of the century.

    Other early stars, such as Buck Ewing, Dan Brouthers, John Clarkson, Hoss Radbourn,
and Tim Keefe, were idolized a century ago. Today, though commemorated in the Hall of
Fame, they've drifted further from common knowledge, replaced in the public's affection by
the stars of the modern (post-1900) era, much as silent movie stars were eclipsed by the
advent of sound.

As baseball's early years drew to a close, the National League faced a threat greater than any it had confronted
before: Rowdyism. This catchall term was insufficient to describe the behavior that increasingly dominated the game
during the 1890s. Players on opposing teams attacked each other; teammates engaged in drunken brawls; fans showered
players with bottles, garbage, and foul language; and everyone teamed up against the umpires, who frequently were lucky
to escape hard-fought games with their lives.

John McGraw and Willie Keeler's Baltimore Orioles, the dominant team of the mid-1890s, were the leading purveyors of rowdyball. They'd break the rules whenever they could get away with it and never hesitated to injure an opposing player or an umpire if doing so would help them win.

Baltimore's fans followed their team's aggressive lead. "That ride in the bus from the ball grounds to the hotel after the first game in Baltimore was the most exciting experience I ever had," Hall of Famer Bobby Wallace told *The Sporting News* in 1895. "The bricks, rocks and chunks of hard slag came through those windows as if shot from a Gatling gun."

By 1900, the sporting press and most of the public were fed up with the rowdyism's antics. Issue after issue of *The Sporting News,* for example, was filled with outraged denunciations of what the game had degenerated into. "ROWDYISM HAS ALMOST RUINED THE PEOPLE'S PASTIME" trumpeted a typical headline.

Some of the owners did attempt to quell on-field behavior. Due to an underlying assumption that fans enjoyed such a spectacle, however, along with the lukewarm disciplinary actions taken by league president Nicholas Young, all efforts were in vain.

Writers and many fans were also disgusted by the trend among league owners to hold interests in more than one team at a time. This habit, called syndicate ownership, enabled the magnates to trade players from their weaker teams to their stronger ones freely during the season. As Bill James puts it, the National League was at the time "a hybrid major/minor league, with teams competing against what would later be called their own farm teams."

Syndicate ownership guaranteed that every season would see second-division teams with embarrassingly bad records finishing fifty or more games out of first place. The infamous Cleveland Spiders of 1899, for example, posted the worst record ever for a major-league team, finishing the season an astounding 20–134.

These unsavory events led to a growing sense of a game no longer accountable to the public, which caused many writers to declare the National League doomed—a possibility not nearly as difficult to imagine then as it would be today. Teams and entire leagues folded all the time; after all, the American Association had succumbed in 1891 and two other short-lived major leagues—the Union (1884) and Players' (1890) leagues—had also come and gone.

The N.L. might easily have gone the way of these other little-remembered leagues of the nineteenth century, if not for the arrival of yet another competitor, this one headed by a man determined to clean up the game. That tough-minded yet visionary man was Ban Johnson, a ballplayer in college, a sportswriter in his youth, a businessman and minor league baseball executive who today is deservedly remembered for none of these accomplishments, but for one more: Saving major league baseball from itself.

THE VIEW FROM GREAT BRITAIN

Quite aware of baseball's immense popularity in the U.S., British writers were concerned about the threat America's game posed to their own national sport, cricket. This concern grew after 1889, when Albert Spalding took the Chicago White Stockings and an all-star team called All America on a world tour that included Egypt (playing a game in front of the pyramids), Australia, and, of course, England. This report, from *Baseball* (1891), by Newton Crane, president of the National Baseball League of Great Britain, captures the prevailing sentiments of the time.

The great baseball tour of 1888–89 took major league baseball to England, Australia, New Zealand—and Egypt.

The first match in London between Chicago and All America was played at the Oval, and attracted from seven to eight thousand spectators. The atmosphere was saturated with moisture, and the fine turf upon which the diagram was laid out was soft and sodden. A fog veiled the outfield, and when a ball was batted in that direction it was immediately lost to sight. Whether the fielder made a catch or not was a matter of conjecture to the on-lookers, who saw nothing beyond the shadowy form of an athlete flying about in the gloom. The base-runners slipped about in the mud and returned to the players' bench covered from head to foot with samples of the soil they had gathered in their round of the bases. Those who understood the game could find but little enjoyment in it, and it was hardly to be expected that those who were unfamiliar with it could view it with pleasure.

The Prince of Wales kindly lent his presence to encourage the promoters of the sport, and remained throughout the contest, taking an apparent interest in every movement of the players. Upon being requested by a newspaper reporter to give his impressions of the game, he asked for the reporter's notebook, and in it wrote the following note, which duly appeared the next morning in the account of the match:—

"The Prince of Wales has witnessed the game of Base Ball with great interest and though he considers it an excellent game he considers Cricket as superior."

A CHANGING GAME

Pre-1900 baseball books and guides paint a picture of the ever-shifting rules of a game that was still coming into focus. The following excerpts contain an endearing combination of ancient rules and strategy modern enough to have been devised yesterday.

The Overworked Catcher
From John Montgomery Ward, *Base-Ball* (1889)

An early "bird cage."

Until within a few years the sign was always given by the pitcher, but now it is almost the universal practice for the catcher to give it to the pitcher. . . . I think the old method was the better, because it is certainly the business of the pitcher not only to do the pitching, but to use his own judgment in deceiving the batsman. . . . Moreover, the catcher has enough of his own to attend to without assuming any of the duties of the pitcher.

The Mind of the Pitcher
From the 1868 *De Witt Guide*

A pitcher is also liable to be annoyed by the foolish and childish habits of some batters in calling for the ball to be delivered at a particular spot, and then asking, "Do you call that here? that's out there," or "way up here"; or being informed that the batter strikes with his bat, and not with his body. . . . Again, batters will make all sorts of pretentious movements for the purpose of annoying a pitcher and deceiving the umpire, by making the latter believe that the former is not delivering the ball fairly. It will be seen, therefore, that to become a first-class pitcher requires continued exercise both of mind and body.

CENTRE FIELDER

A close play at third—with no worries about being spiked.

Opposite: A fully equipped early fly-chaser.

The Stratagem
From John Montgomery Ward, *Base-Ball* (1889)

A pitcher should not be in a hurry to deliver the ball. As soon as the catcher returns the ball the pitcher should assume a position as though about to pitch and stand there; he should take all the time the umpire will give him. This will allow him to give and receive any necessary signal from the catcher, it will rest him and thus enable him to hold his speed, and, finally, it will work upon the nerves and eyesight of the batter. The batter will grow impatient and anxious, and unless his eyes are very strong the long strain in bright light will blear his sight.

The Worst Kind of Hit
From Newton Crane, *Baseball* (1891)

A "swipe," or a "pull," is the worst kind of hit, and the batsman who attempts either should immediately be reproved by his captain. The object in hitting the ball is not to send it up in the air or a long distance in a sky-curve, but to drive it just over the heads of the in-fielders or between them.

A Word for the Beanball
From John Montgomery Ward, *Base-Ball* (1889)

It is amusing to sit in a base-ball crowd and hear the remarks. . . . It would be more amusing still if some of these prodigies could be lifted out of their seats and taken down into the field, and, with a bat in hand, made to face some first-class pitcher until they had hit the ball just once. They would be surprised to see how differently it looks. . . . Just think of it for a moment. A player who can throw a ball, say one hundred and sixteen and two-thirds yards, goes into the pitcher's box and from a distance of only sixteen and two-thirds yards throws the ball to the batter with all speed. If the throw is wild and the ball hits the batter it strikes him with a force that would have been sufficient to carry the ball one hundred yards further. . . . There are a few moments after a man has been hit during which he wishes he had never seen a base-ball, and for the next couple of games, at least, he will think more of escaping a recurrence of the accident than of hitting the ball.

The Right Way to Score a Run
From the *Chadwick Convention Base Ball Manual for 1870*

Opposite: Barely protected, catchers bore the scars of their profession.

Of course his main object is to score a run; but there is something to be considered beside the mere fact of obtaining the run, and that is to secure it with the least fatigue. If the batsman hits the ball over the heads of the out-fielders, he gets his run at once, but at what cost? Why, at the expense of *running one hundred and twenty yards at his utmost speed*, the result being that he arrives home out of breath, and entirely unfit for further play without rest. . . . The science of batting, in fact, lies in that skilful use of the bat which yields the batsman his first base without any extra effort in running.

Above and opposite: Baseball as it used to be: Blue skies, green grass, and bare hands.

Right: The solution and the problem.

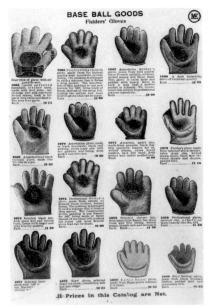

"The Batsman"

From Thomas W. Lawson, *The Krank (His Language and What it Means)* (1888)

> When my willow wand I wave,
>   The fielders like dead men fall;
> Then they hire a train, and start out West,
>   On the trail of the flying ball.

The Origin of the Glove

From Albert G. Spalding, *America's National Game* (1911)

The first glove I ever saw on the hand of a ball player in a game was worn by Charles C. Waite, in Boston, in 1875. He had come from New Haven and was playing at first base. The glove worn by him was of flesh color, with a large, round opening in the back. Now, I had for a good while felt the need of some sort of hand protection for myself. In those days clubs did not carry an extra carload of pitchers, as now. For several years I had pitched in every game played by the Boston team, and had developed severe bruises on the inside of my left hand. When it is recalled that every ball pitched had to be returned, and that every swift one coming my way, from infielders, outfielders or hot from the bat, must be caught or stopped, some idea may be gained of the punishment received.

Therefore, I asked Waite about his glove. He confessed that he was a bit ashamed to wear it, but had it on to save his hand. He also admitted that he had chosen a color as inconspicuous as possible, because he didn't care to attract attention. He added that the opening on the back was for purpose of ventilation.

Meanwhile my own hand continued to take its medicine with utmost regularity, occasionally being bored with a warm twister that hurt excruciatingly. Still, it was not until 1877 that I overcame my scruples against joining the "kid-glove aristocracy" by donning a glove. When I did at last decide to do so, I did not select a flesh-colored glove, but got a black one, and cut out as much of the back as possible to let the air in.

Happily, in my case, the presence of a glove did not call out the ridicule that had greeted Waite. I had been playing so long and had become so well known that the innovation seemed rather to evoke sympathy than hilarity.

1868: THE LAST GASP OF AMATEURISM

By the mid-1860s, the idea of baseball as a game played simply for fun, exercise, or a dream of fair play was admired more in concept than execution. This excerpt from an annotated version of the rules, taken from the 1868 *De Witt Guide,* shows that baseball writers of the time were well aware of what the future would bring.

"Rule V: No players who play base-ball for money shall take part in any match game; and any club giving any compensation to a player, or having, to their knowledge, a player in their nine playing in a match for compensation, shall be debarred from membership in the National Association.". . .

The leading clubs of the country violate [this rule] in the most bare-faced manner, and travel from one point to another as exponents of the beauties of the game, astonishing the clubs with which they come in contact by their wonderful skill, although the fact is patent to everybody that their strength and skill have been gathered and nurtured by their wilful violation of this law.

1869: THE CINCINNATI RED STOCKINGS: BASEBALL'S FIRST DYNASTY

The birth of professional baseball took place in Cincinnati in 1869, when the famed Red Stockings became the first acknowledged all-professional team. Featuring such famous players as Asa Brainard and the brothers Harry and George Wright, the team swept across the country, defeating the best teams that local towns, counties, and cities could muster. The following passages brilliantly convey the tenor of the times—and help explain why baseball would, within a few years, welcome its first major league.

Above: Early player, writer, sporting-goods magnate Albert G. Spalding.

The awe-inspiring 1869 Cincinnati Red Stockings.

An All-Professional Team
From Albert G. Spalding, *America's National Game* (1911)

Before the close of the decade of the 60's there were mutterings of discontent, disparagement, if not of actual disgust with existing conditions. It has already been noted that from the very beginning of Base Ball history betting had been openly, widely, almost generally indulged in at all contests of importance.

Harry Wright (front row, far right) and writer Henry Chadwick (middle row, far right) met as early as 1863 on a team that played both cricket and baseball.

It is unnecessary, perhaps impossible, to catalogue all the evils that followed in the train of this pernicious practice. It is essential to the story, however, to mention the fact that one of the earliest legitimate effects of this illegitimate custom was to beget another practice even more prejudicial to the interests of Base Ball; for betting on the result of games naturally begot collusion between those who bet their money and some of those who played the game. Per consequence, it was soon discovered that unprincipled players, under pretense of accident or inability to make points at critical stages, were "throwing" games.

Nor was this all. The determination of the founders of Base Ball to maintain it as an amateur pastime had been only partially successful from the start. The perfectly natural desire of every club to strengthen its playing corps found its earliest expression in the drafting, by senior clubs, from the ranks of local junior teams the best players among them. This absolutely legitimate practice was soon followed by that of inducing the best players in clubs of small cities and villages to join those of larger cities, the ostensible advantage being set forth as the increased opportunities of getting on in life.

It was, of course, but a very short step from this custom to that of offering to exceptionally good players positions in commercial or industrial enterprises, with the understanding that salaries would be forthcoming. These were usually paid in part by promoters of the ball clubs, and partly by the firms in whose employ the players were enrolled. It was always understood in such cases that, while the player was ostensibly engaged by the house he served, he was really expected to participate in all match games played by the club to which he was to become attached.

It will readily be seen that such a state of things could not long continue. The public lost confidence in a game the results of whose contests depended upon the interests of the gambling fraternity, or the presence of veiled professional players. Upright ball players knew that games were occasionally sold by their unscrupulous companions. Having lost faith in their fellows, they began to lose hope in the future of the pastime itself, and, one by one, conscientious players were dropping out. . . .

Finally one club, actuated by the spirit that has characterized every pioneer movement in history, decided to blaze the way. Consequently, in 1869, under the management of Harry Wright, who had then been playing Base Ball for about ten years, the Cincinnati Red Stockings, formed in 1866 as an amateur team, now determined to organize as an out-and-out professional club, with a view of measuring skill with the heretofore invincible clubs of the East.

This club consisted of trained players, the best men procurable, and every one to receive a substantial salary. The players were Brainard, pitcher; Allison, catcher; Gould, first base; Sweasy, second base; Waterman, third base; George Wright, shortstop; Leonard, left field; Harry Wright, center field; McVey, right field.

A. B. Champion, a prominent lawyer of Cincinnati, was President of the Club, and to him very largely was due the success of the new professional movement.

The Eastern tour of the Red Stockings, in 1869, was preceded by a series of uninterrupted victories over Western clubs. The trip Eastward saw its first contest with the Buffalo Niagaras, after which the Cincinnati Club passed through Western New York to Massachusetts and then to New York City, where they played their first important game with the Mutuals.

Cincinnati's Heroes
From Harry Ellard, *Baseball in Cincinnati* (1907)

The Mutuals of New York, who engaged the Red Stockings in "the best played game of ball on record."

They arrived in New York, Monday evening, June 14, at 8 o'clock, all players fresh and in fine condition, rain having prevented their playing a game with the Yale College nine in the afternoon. Another night's rest, in addition to Sunday's and Monday's leisure, brought the players out as fresh as when they left Cincinnati, and when they arrived at the Union grounds in Brooklyn to fill their engagement with the Mutuals, they were as vigorous, athletic and skillful a body of ballplayers as ever stepped over a ball ground. Aware of the great playing strength of the club, the betting men were exceedingly careful as to how they laid their money, considerable money being invested at low rates, while many bets of $100 to $80 and even $75 were quietly picked up.

The threatening state of the weather kept hundreds away from the grounds, but by 2 P.M., when the game was called, it was estimated that over 10,000 people were present, who watched the game with intense interest within the enclosure, while 1,000 more were gathered upon the housetops overlooking the field and at every loophole where a glimpse of the contestants could be had. Mr. Chas. Walker, of the Active Club, of New York, was chosen as umpire, and the Reds having won the toss, play was called at 3 o'clock, the Mutuals at the bat.

The Mutuals had defeated the great Atlantics, of Brooklyn, and the Athletics, of Philadelphia, and its nine was considered by all Eastern People as invincible. Among its players was Johnny Hatfield, a former Red Stocking, and the longest ball thrower of his day, a magnificent catcher, fine batter and a general all-around, good player. He had been a great favorite in Cincinnati, but through some misunderstanding left the Reds.

There was much ill-feeling toward him by the Cincinnati nine, and Harry Wright had repeatedly told his team that he wanted them, above all things, to beat the Mutuals, and not allow Hatfield under any circumstances to make a run.

The Cincinnatis, up to the time they played the Mutuals, had defeated everything before them. Entire New York pinned its faith in the Mutuals breaking this record. Excitement was at fever heat. At every place where the individual members went before the game they were jeered and hooted at, the general remark being: "Wait till you play the Mutuals," etc. The day the Reds and Mutuals met was one never to be forgotten by those who witnessed the crowds. The streets for miles were packed with people, afoot and in all kinds of vehicles, going to the grounds, and so dense were the spectators on the grounds that the police were fully an hour pushing them back so there could be room for the players. . . .

The game went on amid much cheering, but the most intense excitement prevailed in the ninth inning when the Mutuals went to the bat for the last time. Under ordinary circumstances a lead of one run could have been easily overcome, but, playing as the Cincinnatis did, that one run ahead became of vast importance, and, being whitewashed seven times in succession, the Mutuals themselves had but little confidence in their ability to win.

When the game ended it was considered the best played game of ball on record, both nines playing in a style throughout rarely seen. The most extraordinary stops and catches were made, and although the batting was heavy, but few bases were made.

SCORE OF THE GAME

The great game finished with a score of 4 to 2 to the Reds' favor, and Hatfield never being able to reach first base. The score follows:

Innings	1	2	3	4	5	6	7	8	9		
Mutuals	0	0	0	0	0	0	0	1	1	—	2
Cincinnatis	1	0	1	0	0	0	0	0	2	—	4

When the news of the victory at Brooklyn reached Cincinnati the excitement was beyond description. Salutes were fired, red lights burned and cheers were deafening. Everybody felt in the finest spirits, and many were willing to lend their friends, and even their enemies, any sum without question. Bands were playing all over town and joy reigned supreme. . . .

The club, having defeated the Olympics in a score of 22 to 11, the Athletics in a score of 27 to 18, and the Keystones in a score of 45 to 30, then journeyed to Washington, where they played the Nationals and the Olympics. One of these games was viewed by President Grant. While in Washington all the Reds had an interview with the President, who treated them cordially and complimented them on their play. The President smoked all through the interview. They were treated royally by the members of the two clubs, who took them all around the town, showing them everything of attraction and extending to them every possible courtesy. While going around they sang the song:

> We are a band of baseball players
> From Cincinnati City,
> We come to toss the ball around
> And sing to you our ditty;
> And if you listen to the song
> We are about to sing,
> We'll tell you all about baseball
> And make the welkin ring.
> The ladies want to know
> Who are those gallant men in
> Stockings red, they'd like to know.

The Washington papers stated, "The Cincinnati Club drew the most aristocratic assemblage at its games that ever put in an appearance at a baseball match."

The next stop was at Wheeling, W. Va., where it played the Baltic Club, and thence back home, arriving in Cincinnati from its great, successful Eastern Tour on Thursday, July 1.

The triumphant Red Stockings, returning from their undefeated eastern tour, receive a hero's welcome and an enormous trophy bat.

The reception given the players was long to be remembered. They were met by all the members of the club with a band and escorted through the streets, which were decorated on all sides. One firm made a unique design of the letter C of red stockings. Cheer upon cheer went up for the invincible champions, and pandemonium reigned throughout the town. The next day the club played a picked nine for an exhibition game. When the game was completed a wagon drove onto the field with a huge bat, in shape the same as a regular bat, but it was twenty-seven feet long, nineteen inches at the butt and nine and one-half inches at the wrist. On the side was painted "Champion Bat," in gilt, while underneath were handsomely inscribed all the names of the players of 1869.

It was presented by the Cincinnati Lumber Company, and the presentation speech was made by Carter Gazley, the secretary of the company, in which he stated that "the Cincinnati Baseball Club players were recognized as the heaviest batters in the country, and, on that account, it gave him much pleasure to present them with a bat which, although not of regulation size, was not so heavy but that they could easily handle it." He also said that it was not purchased from Geo. B. Ellard, but was grown to order for the occasion. . . .

THE REDS OF SIXTY-NINE
By Harry Ellard

An old man sat in his easy-chair,
    Smoking his pipe of clay,
Thinking of years when he was young,
    Thus whiling his hours away.
Thinking when he was but a boy,
    So full of mirth and glee,
And we hear him say: "How things have changed;
    They are not as they used to be.

"When I was young, and played baseball
    With the Reds of Sixty-nine,
We then knew how to play the game;
    We all were right in line.

"We used no mattress on our hands,
    No cage upon our face;
We stood right up and caught the ball
    With courage and with grace.

"And when our bats would fan the air
    You bet we'd make a hit;
The ball would fly two hundred yards
    Before it ever lit.

"A home run all could easily make,
    And sometimes six or eight;

Each player knew his business then
    As he stepped up to the plate.

"Let's see! There's Leonard and George Wright,
    And Sweasy and McVey
With Brainard and Fred Waterman—
    These men knew how to play.

"'Doug' Allison, too, could bat in style,
    And so could Charlie Gould,
While Harry Wright oft said with pride,
    'My boys are never fooled.'

"The game you see them play to-day
    Is tame as it can be;
You never hear of scores like ours—
    A hundred and nine to three.

"Well, well, my boy, those days are gone;
    No club will ever shine
Like the one which never knew defeat,
    The Reds of Sixty-Nine."

"The Birth of a New Era"
From Albert G. Spalding, *America's National Game* (1911)

This sensational record, without a parallel then, has never been equalled. Aside from its spectacular effect, in calling attention to the great players of a great club and their wonderful achievements, it exerted a tremendous influence, afterwards to be felt in the game itself, for it portended the birth of a new era in which professional ball should become thoroughly established, though not without its serious vicissitudes.

The Red Stockings had now played every prominent club from Massachusetts to California without losing a game, and this wonderful succession of victories was continued not only through 1869, but also from April to June in 1870, without a defeat.

From a record kept by Harry Wright, the great captain and manager of the Red Stockings, the following facts concerning that club, its players and its record are gleaned: Out of 57 games played the Red Stockings won 56 and tied 1. In these games they scored a total of 2,395 runs to 574 for their adversaries. The nature of the batting done is shown in a total of 169 home runs, or an average of nearly three to a game. The number of miles traveled by rail and boat was 11,877, without a serious accident of any kind. Over 200,000 people witnessed the games. The individual score of George Wright, the famous shortstop, was the highest of any player on the team. He played in 52 of the 57 games. His batting average was .518. He made 339 runs, of which 59 were home runs; one of them the longest hit up to that time.

Such is the story of the first professional Base Ball club, as taken from the records. Aside from the achievements of the Red Stockings during their brief but meteoric career, it will not be easy to estimate the influence of their performances upon the future of the game. The club, as organized by Harry Wright, passed out of existence in the fall of 1870, but it had paved the way for the introduction of new means, new measures, new methods, soon inaugurated, and which are an integral part of the system to-day.

"BASE-BALL AMONG THE SOUTHERNERS"

The mushrooming popularity of baseball was not only a Northern phenomenon in the years after the Civil War. The following, from the 1869 *De Witt Guide,* shows that the game was important in attempts to reunite a shattered nation.

The call to arms reaches the ballfield, 1861.

There is probably nothing the youth of the South have so long been in need of, in the way of healthy recreation, as some outdoor sport which would afford alike a legitimate field for the cultivation of those inherent attributes of manliness which characterize Southerners so much, and an exercise suitable to the climate in which they live. With every requisite to excel in any game in which people of more temperate climes are skilled, they have been obliged until within a few years past, to allow their athletic powers to lie dormant from lack of opportunity to cultivate them to advantage. The

Baseball during the Civil War, a valuable distraction from harsh realities.

time has arrived, however, when we are to see the last, we trust, of that listlessness and love of indolent pleasures which has too long been a blot on the escutcheon of Southern youths. The late war proved conclusively their powers of physical endurance, as it did the courage, pluck and nerve which they can bring to bear in their efforts to accomplish any task in which their hearts are engaged; and now that peace once more reigns in the land, and that the factionists of both sections of the country are daily giving ground before the advancing steps of a social as well as political reformation, and manly games and trials of athletic skill have taken the place of the bloody contests on the field of battle, we hope to see the manly qualifications we have alluded to, developed to an extent hitherto unknown in the annals of the South.

With the lack of opportunity for a full development of the inherent ability of the Southern youth, to excel in athletic games and exercises, there has been a sad want experienced of those attractions belonging to the out-door sports of "Merrie England," which have made the rosy-cheeked belles of the nobility of the "sea-girt isle" models of healthy beauty. The ladies of the South have too long been deprived of every avenue of out-door exercise and recreation—save equestrianism—which is now open to, and so frequented by the fashionable belles of the North. Skating, with its joyous exhilaration, their climate excludes them from enjoying, but croquet and base-ball afford them, on the one hand, a recreation, in which they can actively participate, and on the other, a most exciting and attractive sport which they can patronize and enjoy without the slightest fear of encountering an objectionable word or action calculated to offend the most fastidious. Henceforth the fair dames and damsels of the South will smile on the champions of the ball-field, as their ancestry were wont to do upon those who "on faire steeds and in gallant forme," so proudly charged with lance in rest, upon their adversary of the olden time tournament. In fact, what cricket is for noble dames of England, to grace with their presence, so is base-ball for the patronage of the refined and cultivated classes of the fair belles of America, North and South alike.

During the war the many games of base-ball played by the Northern soldiers on the camp fields and on some of the prison grounds, led to the introduction of the game among the Southern soldiers, and "when the cruel war was over," the game was generally adopted throughout the South; the students of the University of Virginia being among the advance guard of the Southern army of the fraternity, and as whatever Old Virginia takes the lead in, her sisters of the South generally follow, the game has now assumed a popularity from Richmond to New Orleans, which makes it quite the rage of the season.

In conclusion we have simply to state that unlike most of the furores which characterize our people North and South alike, this passion for so manly a pastime and healthy an exercise is one that possesses the most advantages and the least objectionable features of anything we have ever before had a furore for.

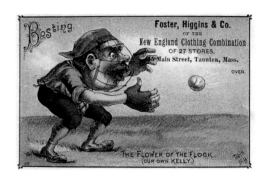

Mike "King" Kelly, "the Flower of the Flock," whose exploits on the field kept league officials changing the rules to control him.

1882: KING KELLY EARNS HIS REPUTATION

Perhaps the most famous nineteenth-century star was Mike "King" Kelly, a witty man and creative ballplayer who helped build his own legend as he led Cap Anson's Chicago White Sox to dominate the National League in the early 1880s. Kelly would take advantage of the era's single umpire per game to sneak from first to third (without touching second) on a base hit. As this story, from Kelly's 1888 *Play Ball: Stories of the Diamond Field,* shows, he wasn't averse to bending the rules in other ways, too.

A moment of uncharacteristic repose for King Kelly.

The Chicago club always had to play a pretty stiff game of ball to win from the other league clubs. There was always more or less feeling against the nine in various quarters, probably because they were such great kickers at times. However, the boys didn't mind this very much: in fact they enjoyed it. It spurred them on, sometimes, to play great ball. I think the three most exciting games of ball I ever played in were against the Providence team, at Chicago, in 1882. The games practically settled which nine was to wave the championship pennant. The Providence club came to Chicago, four games ahead of the White Stocking nine. George and Harry Wright were two of the first members of the club that I met near the dressing-room. Harry was the manager of the Providence club then, and George was the short-stop. The latter was a great short-stop. He picked up a ball with great neatness and dexterity. He was a good, safe thrower, and seldom, indeed, did he make a mistake. A very gentlemanly fellow, both on and off the ball field, he had a good many friends, both in and out of the base ball profession. He is now in business in Boston with Henry Ditson, a bright young fellow, who is a great lover of lawn tennis.

Both the Wrights were confident that Chicago would drop three straight games to the Providence boys, and that they would win the championship. I wanted to bet Harry a new hat, but he wouldn't bet. The first game was the most hotly contested game of ball I ever played in. Every point was fought, and each man exerted every effort to have his side win. We, perhaps, had a little the best of it, in view of the fact that we were at home, and were sure to get the encouragement of the thousands of spectators who witnessed the game. The score in the last inning was four to three in favor of the Providence club. There was one man out when I scratched a hit. I got on first and was about to make an attempt to steal second, when Burns, who followed me, hit a hot grounder to George Wright. There was one player out, and if George ever got the ball to second it meant a double play, and that would settle the game. Instead of fielding the ball to the second baseman, he started for the bag himself. I never ran so hard in my life. I reached the bag a second before George, and then like a flash, he raised his arm to send the ball to the first base, to cut off Burns. Somehow or other an accident occurred at that moment. My arm went up in the air, and it caught George on the shoulder. The result was that when the ball left George's hand it went away over into the grand stand. I scored first, and Burns followed me a moment later. The cheers from a thousand enthusiastic spectators proved that the Chicago club had won the first great game. The next two were afterwards won by us, and in the ten games that followed with other clubs, Providence won but two.

Harry Wright was the maddest man in Chicago when the series had finished, and he claimed that were it not for "Kelly and his infernal tricks," the Providence club would have won the series and the championship. He swore that he would have revenge in the future. I saw him, and had quite a talk with him. I said, "Mr. Wright, I have played ball for a number of years; I will do everything in the world to win a championship game of ball. That is what I am paid for. But during all the time I have played ball, I never hurt a player. I never spiked a man, never knocked a man down. I play ball to win, and if I have to employ a few subterfuges to win I cannot help it. I wouldn't wilfully hurt George Wright, or any man in your club. But self-preservation is the law of nature. When I saw George raise his arm, I knew that if something didn't occur we would be defeated. I didn't think of George nor myself. I simply thought of the Chicago club." Harry was smiling before I finished, and he was willing to forgive me. Instead of having revenge, he has been a good friend of mine since that time.

1883: THE CHANGING OF THE GUARD

The 1880s were a time of constant experimentation with baseball rules. While many changes were engineered by National League executives, the players on the field appear to have taken the lead in abandoning the rule that required them to throw the ball underhand. Despite the following lamentation, first published in the 1884 *Spalding Guide,* once the era's pitchers realized how hard they could throw overhand, they never looked back.

But little if any advance was made in the art of strategic pitching in 1883, the overhand throwing prevailing to an extent which materially interfered with progress in strategic skill. Some of our readers may naturally inquire, "What is strategic pitching?" and the answer is that it is the art of out-manoeuvering the batsman, by puzzling his judgment and deceiving his eyesight; in plain words it is the skill which leads him to think that the very ball he likes to hit is coming from the pitcher, when in reality it is a ball he cannot hit successfully. The essentials of strategic pitching are, first, thorough command of the ball in delivery; second, the skill to disguise a marked change of pace; third, to try and get the batsman out of form for hitting, and when he is so to send the ball in "over the plate" and at the height called for. These points of play, combined with a judicious use of the "curves," and of a swift delivery—the latter according to the ability of the catcher only—constitute the elements of strategic pitching, and it is this style of pitching, and this only, which will eventually supersede all others as the game approaches the point of perfect play. Toward the close of the season of 1883 overhand throwing prevailed almost entirely in the professional arena, the rule prohibiting it being ignored alike by the umpires and by the pitchers.

THE SHAPE OF THINGS TO COME: PLAYER VS. WRITER

This passage appeared in the May 10, 1886, issue of *The Sporting News,* sounding a note that resounds today.

No two professions are so allied together as that of the base ball writer and player, and yet, as a matter of fact, the bond of friendship between the two is of the frailest kind. Few ball players who read the humorous or regular incidents of the game pause to picture the patient man with pen or pencil sitting down to body them forth. He is hidden, with few exceptions, behind his work, and aims so to hide himself. His pen is oftener dipped in the milk of human kindness than in gall, and yet the good things he does are passed by unnoticed, while the ill are remembered for all time. You may speak well of this player and that, pat them on the back, send their name flying from one end of the continent to the other, making their reputation world wide if you will, but once chronicle their shortcomings and all the good things you have said of them are forgotten. On the other hand, it may happen that the young chronicler of the game is too quick to find fault and too ready to pick flaws in the work of this player or that. Such cases are frequent, to say the least and but serve to widen the breach. One thing is certain, however, and that is that the time must come when the player and the writer on base ball will be better and closer friends than they are now. One is as much interested in the success of the game as the other, and when all come to learn this fact there will be better feeling all around and a more lasting bond of friendship than there is now.

THE MAKING OF A BALLPLAYER: CAP ANSON

Cap Anson, the great Chicago White Stocking star, accrued 3000 hits and a .329 lifetime batting average in a twenty-two-year-long career that landed him in the Hall of Fame. He also wrote baseball's first true autobiography, *A Ballplayer's Career* (1900). In the excerpt that follows, the Marshalltown, Iowa, native describes a temptation that confronted him once his fame as a ballplayer began to spread throughout the state.

Cap Anson, star player-manager with the Chicago White Stockings, 1876–97.

A feeling of most intense rivalry in the base-ball line existed between Des Moines and Clinton, Iowa, and one time when the former had a match on with the latter I received an offer of fifty dollars from the Clinton team to go on there and play with them in a single game.

Now fifty dollars at that time was more money than I had ever had at any one time in my life, and so without consulting any one I determined to accept the offer. I knew that I would be compelled to disguise myself in order to escape recognition either by members of the Des Moines team or by some of the spectators, and this I proceeded to do by dying my hair, staining my skin, etc.

The 1879 Chicago White Stockings, with Cap Anson (far left) and Albert G. Spalding (center, with walking stick).

Opposite: The young Cap Anson.

Overleaf: The St. Louis Browns, the first dynasty of the upstart American Association.

I did not think that my own father could recognize me, when I completed my preparations and started to the depot to take the train for Des Moines, but that was where I made a mistake. The old gentleman ran against me on the platform, penetrated my disguise at once and asked me where I was going. I told him, and then he remarked that I should do no such thing, and he started me back home in a hurry. When he got there he gave me a lecture, told me that such a proceeding on my part was not honest and would ruin my reputation. In fact, he made me thoroughly ashamed of myself. The team from Clinton had to get along without my services, but I shall never forget what a time I had in getting the dye out of my hair and the stain from my skin.

That fifty dollars that I didn't get bothered me, too, for a long time afterwards. I am glad now, however, that the old gentleman prevented me getting it. Dishonesty does not pay in base-ball any better than it does in any other business, and that I learned the lesson early in life is a part of my good fortune.

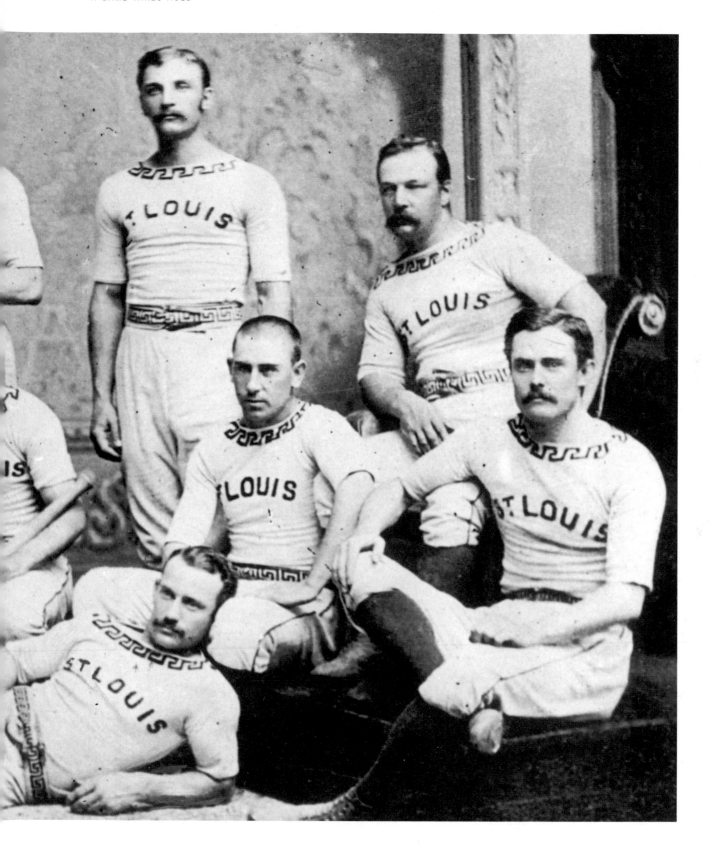

1886: THE FIRST GREAT "WORLD SERIES"

A temporary alliance between the National League and the upstart American Association allowed the playing of the first championship series in the early and mid-1880s. The best of these took place in 1886 and resulted in victory for the American Association's St. Louis Browns over the Chicago White Stockings. Compare the casual nature of the game arrangements, as reported in the October 11, 1886, *Sporting News,* with the rigorously planned big-business precision of today's World Series.

The 1885 American Association champion St. Louis Browns, with owner Chris von der Ahe (left inset) and player-manager Charlie Comiskey (right inset).

All week Messrs. Von der Ahe and Spalding, respectively the presidents of the St. Louis and Chicago clubs, have been at work arranging for their series of games for the championship of the world. Early in the week the two compromised on the number of games to be played. It will be remembered that when Mr. Von der Ahe first challenged the Chicagos, he named five as the number of games to be played. Mr. Spalding in his response named nine. Later they compromised on six games, with the understanding that if they should tie on threes, then an extra, or seventh game should be played on some neutral ground. . . .

The arrangement of the world series interfered somewhat with the local series between the Browns and Maroons, but on Wednesday last Messrs. Stromberg and O'Connell met Mr. Von der Ahe, and the result was a friendly controversy in which both sides made concessions. . . .

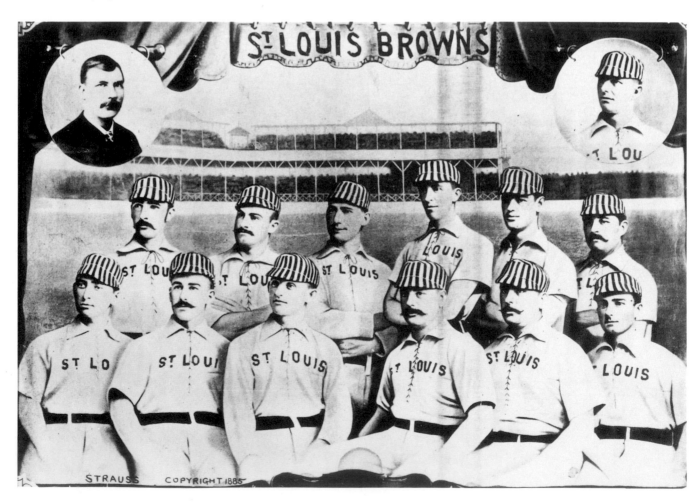

THE COLOR LINE DESCENDS

While it's common knowledge that in 1947 Jackie Robinson became the first black ballplayer to break through the major league color barrier, he was not the first black man to play in the majors. Moses Fleetwood Walker, who had caught for Oberlin College, played with Toledo of the American Association in 1884, while his brother, Weldy, also made a brief appearance with Toledo. But, as this heartbreaking excerpt from *Sol White's Official Base Ball Guide* (1907) shows, by the late 1880s racism was on the rise—and at least one early superstar was an eager supporter of a barrier that would last sixty years.

In 1887 no less than twenty colored ball players scattered among the different smaller leagues of the country. . . . But this year marked the beginning of the elimination of colored players from white clubs. All the leagues, during the Winter of 1887 and 1888, drew the color line, or had a clause inserted in their constitutions limiting the number of colored players to be employed by each club.

This color line had been agitated by A. C. [Cap] Anson, Captain of the Chicago National League team for years. . . . Were it not for this same man Anson there would have been a colored player in the National League in 1887. John M. Ward, of the New York club, was anxious to secure Geo. Stovy and arrangements were about completed for his transfer from the Newark club, when a howl was heard from Chicago to New York. This same Anson . . . made strenuous and fruitful opposition to any proposition looking to the admittance of a colored man into the National League. Just why Adrian C. Anson, manager and captain of the Chicago National League Club, was so strongly opposed to colored players on white teams cannot be explained. His repugnant feeling, shown at every opportunity, toward colored ball players, was a source of comment throughout every league in the country, and his opposition, with his great popularity and power in base ball circles, hastened the exclusion of the black man from the white leagues.

THE BALTIMORE ORIOLES: BEST TEAM OF THE 1890S

The most famous—or notorious—team of the 1890s was the Baltimore Orioles, which included such still-familiar names as John McGraw and Willie Keeler. The following excerpt comes from *The Great Teams of Baseball,* by MacLean Kennedy, which takes a hero-worshiping tone typical of many baseball books early in this century. But in its description of John McGraw, it alluded to what true fans knew and contemporary newspaper and magazine accounts reported: The Orioles not only played hard—they played dirty. Led by McGraw, they were the leading proponents of rowdyball, whose methods included spiking opposing players, harassing the umpires, and breaking any rule they could get away with in order to win. And win they did, capturing three successive pennants in 1894–96.

It was a great record the Baltimore team created from 1894 until 1898, inclusive. Three firsts and two seconds, made in a 12-club circuit, is touching the phenomenal. During that period the team played 666 games, winning 452, a percentage in games won of .678. It was a genuine never-say-die aggregation. It was a team always pulling off the unexpected, never linking to any particular style of play. The Orioles were the inventors of the hit-and-run and the sacrifice game. . . .

*The notorious 1894 Baltimore
Orioles, whose playing style, claimed
team member Wilbert Robinson,
wasn't rowdyism: "It was the
earnestness born of rare zeal."*

John McGraw played third base. He played other positions, but third base was the position assigned to him after he became a big league player. John J. wasn't the most brilliant fielding third sacker the game ever had, for his lifetime average in fielding in the position stood .895. Jimmy Collins and Lave Cross, during the same period, had lifetime averages of .930 or better. But Mac was there other ways. He was the most effective and clever base stealer, and run-getter, batsman, inside-stuff exponent and rough stuff artist that the big league had at that time or since.

McGraw didn't do the stereotyped, cut-and-dried stuff one sees in every-day base running. McGraw, like Cobb, seemed to be inspired when on the base lines—actually inspired by existing conditions. His work on the lines was spontaneous. Catchers, pitchers and basemen used to watch him so closely that they became plainly nervous. Like the famous Cobb, the star of the old Oriole team didn't lead in the number of bases stolen for all time. Something like 500 was his record, and the best he did for a single season was 77, but it was the mere appearance of the scrappy one on the base lines that caused apprehension.

WILLIE KEELER'S LAMENT

But even a team as potent as the Orioles could not be successful forever. In a lament that could be transferred wholesale to the mouth of any modern player, Willie Keeler bids farewell to the Oriole powerhouse that was no more. From *Sporting Life,* October 22, 1898.

"For four years we laughed at the pitchers and the other teams in the League, but now they are laughing at us," remarked Willie Keeler in the West the other day. "There was a time when we got into a town that four or five of the home team's pitchers would complain of lame arms and sore shoulders. It is different now. When we walk out on the field five or six pitchers are anxious to get at us. They fight to pitch against us, for they know that we are easy. We could not hit barn doors if they were pitching them over, but that's the way it goes in base ball. You're a king one day and a lobster the next."

Taking a page from the Orioles' book, other 1890s teams—and their fans—showed no mercy to the overmatched umpires.

ROWDYISM: THE PLAGUE THAT ALMOST RUINED THE GAME

The Orioles were the leading proponents of rowdy play, but far from its only practitioners. As the century drew to a close, the National League and many smaller leagues were rife with violent language and behavior—aimed by players and fans alike at other players, managers, writers, and, particularly, umpires, who went through a decade that must have made them wish they'd chosen another line of work. Obscene and threatening language was so common that women rarely attended games, and physical assaults were amazingly frequent.

Henry Chadwick, nineteenth-century baseball's most revered writer, fan, and philosopher, was obviously horrified by the slew of unsavory incidents. The following excerpts, from newspaper accounts of the 1880s and '90s, are taken from clippings in Chadwick's unpublished diaries and hint at the extent of the problem throughout organized baseball.

"Unless summary action is taken by the league, the national game will speedily degenerate into rough and tumble, eye gouging, and head breaking contests," warned the Brooklyn Eagle.

CHICAGO—Jimmy Ryan last night after the game assaulted a reporter of the *Evening News* named Geo. Bechel. The latter had criticized Ryan and when he appeared in the club-house after the game Ryan picked a quarrel with him. He then attacked him, using him up pretty badly.

NEW ORLEANS—At a game of baseball in Carrollton yesterday afternoon the decision of the umpire produced ill feeling, and Gabe Jones, the manager of the Allen Baseball Club, whipped out his revolver and opened fire on the crowd, killing Robert Jones, a spectator, instantly, and seriously wounding Louis Foster and Richard Williams. James Brook, manager of the opposing club, the Wilson Bas-ball [*sic*] Club, fired at Jones, but was a bad marksman and hit no one. A general fight ensued and a number of persons were injured, none seriously.

CINCINNATI—During the game to-day, Ward and Robinson, becoming angered at the umpire (who was perfectly right in his decision), stood in front of the grand stand filled with ladies and uttered oaths and curses until a number of ladies left the stand. In the fourth inning, when a run looked promising for Cincinnati, Vickery threw a ball with extra deliberation and speed, aimed at Harry Vaughn. It hit him on the arm and it is feared the arm is broken. It was palpably intentional.

NEW YORK—Eddie Burke, the erratic left fielder of the New York Baseball Club, has been in trouble again. He has partially recovered from a severe thrashing at the hands of Second Baseman "Jack" Doyle, also of the New Yorks. The trouble, which took place last Thursday night in an Eighth Avenue saloon, near 145th Street, has been kept very quiet. Up to yesterday Burke has been nursing his bruises at home.

SYRACUSE, NY—The baseball season closed here to-day with a disgraceful scene on the diamond. In the sixth inning, when the score was tied, Harper got caught between the bases, and by the dirtiest trick ever witnessed in this city he reached second. Harper deliberately jumped upon Moss, who had the ball ready to touch him, and he spiked the Stars' short stop so hard in the breast that his shirt front was torn almost into ribbons. Moss struck Harper with his fist, and a rough-and-tumble fight would have ensued but for police interference.

LOUISVILLE—Yesterday's game proved an expensive one for the Cleveland Club, for warrants were issued this afternoon for the arrest of Cuppy, O'Connor, Tebeau, Childs, McKean, McGarr, Burkett, McAleer, and Blake. . . . The evidence tended to show that the players of both teams had indulged in "dirty ball play." It was shown, however, that after the game the treatment of Umpire Weidman on the part of the Cleveland players had been abusive, and of a nature to incite a riot. Several witnesses also testified that Tebeau, McKean, and O'Connor had used vile epithets, while McAleer had struck the umpire.

BROOKLYN—Unless summary action is taken by the league, the national game will speedily degenerate into rough and tumble, eye gouging and head breaking contests, in which the innings will be called rounds and the abilities of the players will be judged by their slugging propensities. The magnates are themselves to blame by paving the way for the Tebeau episode, in which that player resorted to disgraceful methods and then set the entire league at defiance.

Yesterday, another row occurred at Pittsburgh, which will also go unpunished because the courts are open for the protection of the offending players and the hands of the officials are tied. According to a dispatch from Pittsburgh, the game was close and the home team was one run in the lead until Philadelphia went to bat in the last inning. They batted Hastings for three runs and took the lead with two to spare. In Pittsburgh's half the local men filled the bases on a close decision with only one out. Philadelphia kicked hard on the decisions, and while the players were having it out with

Players, managers, fans—
no one at the ballpark was safe.

The hot-headed Patsy Tebeau.

the umpire, Ely scored from third. This further enraged the visitors. Taylor struck the umpire and Clements was only prevented from doing so by Nash, who ran out on the field from the bench. Taylor and Clements were both fined and removed from the game, Carsey and Grady taking their places. Carsey made a balk, allowing another run and tying the score. Then the visitors all gathered about the umpire again, and the police had to be called. When quiet was restored Beckley singled, and the winning run was scored. Nothing like it was ever seen on the local grounds.

PART TWO

1901-1920:
THE MODERN ERA BEGINS

The piercing gaze of disciplinarian Ban Johnson.

If ever a time in professional baseball has proven the game's resiliency—its ability to survive many and diverse threats—the period that began at the turn of the century and culminated at the close of the 1920 season was the one. Though besieged both early and late by forces that seemed likely to torpedo it, somehow the game survived. And it didn't just survive, but it thrived, featuring some of the most unforgettable stars, finest play, and greatest pennant races and World Series in baseball history.

By 1900, the evils of rowdyism and syndicate ownership and the resulting financial debacles among many teams had left the N.L. in critical condition. In a belated attempt to deal with these problems, the League dropped a third of its franchises (including the poor Cleveland Spiders) after the 1899 season, leaving eight teams to struggle into the new century.

But soon thereafter, the League received another blow to its stability: The 1900 founding of the Players' Protective Association, a union born from player objections to the reserve clause, which forced them to stay with one team (virtually always at whatever salary was offered them) at the whim of the owners. The Association also objected to players having no influence over where they were traded or sold, and not benefiting from the proceeds of such sales. Not surprisingly, the N.L. was far from receptive to the new organization's demands.

Taking advantage of player discontent and the N.L.'s shaky finances, Ban Johnson made his move—and his goal wasn't to save the established league, but to compete with it. Johnson, as president of the minor Western League, had already proven his ability to run a financially successful league, but now he wanted more.

Beginning after the 1899 season, Johnson, backed by former-ballplayer-turned-business-executive Charles Comiskey and other wealthy and self-confident compatriots, made several moves to strengthen his minor league. He renamed it the American League, placed franchises in Chicago, Cleveland, and other big cities, and publicized the fact that *his* league refused to permit the evils so entrenched in N.L. play.

Before taking the final step of declaring his organization a major league, however, Johnson expressed a wish to attend the N.L.'s annual meeting in New York and negotiate an alliance. Instead, the N.L.'s magnates allowed him to wait fruitlessly in Philadelphia. "The message the owners sent him was negative," points out Eugene C. Murdock in *Ban Johnson: Czar of Baseball* (1982). "'They sent back word,' Ban recalled, 'that I could stay there until hell froze over.'"

Soon after this slight, Johnson took the battle to the older league, moving franchises to such larger eastern cities as Boston and Philadelphia, where they were in direct competition with established N.L. teams. In addition, he took advantage of player unrest following the N.L.'s rejection of many of the Players' Protective Association's demands by offering more flexible contracts and more money than did the N.L., which had a salary ceiling of $2400 per player, and paid most far less.

These tactics allowed the new league to woo and sign such stars as Cy Young, Sam Crawford, John McGraw, Nap Lajoie, and Mike Donlin. "In the meantime the owners of the National League clubs sat calmly by with a feeling of security that the clause in their contracts giving them an option on a player for two years would be sustained by the courts," commented the 1902 *Spalding Guide*.

The best seats in the house for the first true World Series: Boston-Pittsburgh, 1903.

Standing room only in Boston's Huntington Grounds for the last game of the 1903 Series. In early important games, crowds were allowed to overflow onto the field.

But by the end of the 1902 season, the courts had refused to intervene, and it was clear to everyone that the American League was here to stay—and was, in fact, in many ways already the more successful league. Peace arrived in the form of an alliance between equals in 1903, with the two leagues agreeing to abide by each other's contracts and rights to players. The Players' Protective Association, used so effectively by Johnson, now found itself ignored and soon dissolved.

The new alliance produced at least one immediate benefit: The first true World Series, a 1903 battle between the A.L.'s Boston Red Sox (also known as the Pilgrims) and the N.L.'s Pittsburgh Pirates. The Red Sox, behind Cy Young and Big Bill Dineen, beat the Pirates five games to three, proving once and for all that the A.L. belonged on the same stage with the senior circuit. The series was also famous for Boston's Royal Rooters' incessant singing of "Honus, Why Do You Hit So Badly" (sung to the tune of a popular song, "Tessie, You Know I Love You Madly"), which drove Honus Wagner to such distraction that the Hall of Fame shortstop hit a mere .222 for the Series.

With a single time-out in 1904 (when the N.Y. Giants' owner John Brush and manager John McGraw refused to play the Red Sox), the World Series soon began to excite great interest among baseball fans and the press, becoming one of the reasons why attendance boomed in both leagues as the decade progressed. Just as important was Johnson's success at controlling rowdyball in the A.L., with the N.L. following suit within a few years. While of course rowdyism never disappeared entirely, the new cleaner game made going to the ballpark an acceptable diversion once more, even for women.

IF IT
HASN'T
THIS
LABEL

MADE FOR THE
B.V.D.
BEST RETAIL TRADE

IT
ISN'T
B.V.D.
UNDERWEAR

Thos. Cusack Company

KUPPENHEIMER CLOTHES
SOLD EXCLUSIVELY BY
Brill Brothers

IN 1917 BURNS N.Y. CAUGHT

But perhaps the central reason for baseball's fat years in the early 1900s was also the most obvious: The players. Rarely has there been a gallery of stars so diverse, colorful, and talented as those who blossomed at the beginning of the modern era.

What was particularly interesting were the contrasts presented by many of the greatest players. Ty Cobb was a violent, paranoid man who also happened to be one of the greatest hitters of all time; another was Honus Wagner, beloved for his cheerful disposition and kindness to other players. Joe Jackson's lack of learning was considered to be part of his charm, while Christy Mathewson combined matinee-idol looks with All-American-boy intelligence. But there was no counterpart to George Herman Ruth—the Big Bam, the Babe, who emerged in this era as a brilliant young pitcher for the Boston Red Sox, but who would leave an everlasting mark in later years, in a different city, with a bat in his hands.

Cleveland second baseman Nap Lajoie, the sixth player named to the Hall of Fame.

Opposite: The New York Giants raising the N.L. pennant, the Polo Grounds, 1917.

Nor were these the only stars of the time. Walter Johnson, Nap Lajoie, Sam Crawford, Three Finger Brown, Cy Young, Tris Speaker—each name, still famous today, called to mind an instantly recognizable pitching motion, batting stance, or running style to the era's fans.

But even as baseball thrived on the field, new threats were emerging to its popularity and prosperity. Attendance, after booming between 1900 and 1909, began to decline. Then, in 1914, it collapsed, falling by nearly a third in a single year.

One reason that the game seemed to fall so dramatically out of favor was the arrival of the Federal League as a direct competitor in 1914. Using an updated form of the tactics employed by Ban Johnson years earlier, the Feds placed teams in cities that allowed them to compete directly with the two established leagues. They also "stole" players with large salary offers and bonuses, as well as promises of more liberal contracts that gave the players more control over their futures. Players jumped from league to league, seeking the best possible deal for themselves; meanwhile, the new and old leagues went after each other in court.

For two years salaries boomed. Then, when the Federal League folded after the 1915 season, a victim of too many baseball teams vying for fans disgusted by the ongoing legal and financial battles, the players suddenly found themselves with nowhere to go but the two established leagues. Players who had jumped to the Feds were allowed back, at pre–Federal League salaries, of course, and without any of the other benefits they'd enjoyed so briefly.

The players had no choice but to accept the return of the old rules. It's impossible, though, to overstate the effect two years of comparative freedom must have had on players who, for a brief moment, were treated as well as they thought they deserved to be treated. Following the death of the Federal League, the resentment among the players was palpable. Their anger doomed the Players' Fraternity, a group founded in 1912 whose goal had been to negotiate better conditions with the owners, but which was perceived as moving too slowly and ineffectively. More importantly, the players' growing sense of injustice led directly (and, perhaps, inexorably) to the catastrophe of the so-called Black Sox scandal.

As is well known by now, in 1919 a group of Chicago White Sox stars, including such potential Hall of Famers as Joe Jackson and Eddie Cicotte, accepted money from gamblers to throw the World Series against the Cincinnati Reds. The full extent of the scandal didn't unfold until the end of the troubled 1920 season—already tainted by the shocking death of Ray Chapman after being struck by a Carl Mays pitch—but today at least some of its causes seem clear: The White Sox were a tremendously successful and popular team whose wealthy owner, Charles Comiskey, paid notoriously low wages (even for the time). Jackson, Cicotte, and the rest of the corrupted players felt no loyalty to an owner who treated them badly, and they leaped at the opportunity to earn money another way—even if it meant letting down their honest teammates.

Not that the Black Sox scandal exploded without warning. Rumors of players "laying down"—losing games for pay—had been circulating for years. Yet league officials lacked the energy or will to confront the charges, unmask the culprits, and send a message that major league baseball was clean.

Many of the rumors focused on Hal Chase, who played for five teams between 1905 and 1919. One of the best first basemen of the time, Chase seems to have been corrupting his teammates and fixing games as early as 1908 and was accused repeatedly by his managers of throwing or attempting to throw games. Somehow he always managed to

Opposite and above: The Brooklyn Tip-Tops and Buffalo Blues of the Federal League. For two seasons, the Feds gave players large salaries and a measure of freedom.

beat the charges. "He is a curious individual and he makes strange remarks," admitted *Baseball Magazine* of Chase, but added that "[i]n this country a man is innocent until he is proved guilty."

Then came the great 1919 fix, which Chase, a bad penny if ever there was one, apparently helped set up. Before the Series even began, writers, players, and others heard the rumors that something untoward was taking place—rumors that seemed convincing to all but the heads of organized baseball. Rather than undertaking a vigorous investigation, league officials and their supporters in the press spent a year stridently attacking the credentials and character of anyone who suggested that the Series might have been crooked.

Then, when incontrovertible evidence of the fix began to appear, the owners suddenly found themselves facing the real possibility that the game might never regain its popularity with disgusted and distrustful fans. Major league baseball, which had survived so many threats in its first fifty years, seemed on the verge of being eaten away from the inside.

Something had to be done to restore the game's integrity. But what?

1901: THE BIG STICK OF BAN JOHNSON

Despite countless attempts, by 1901 the National League had proven itself unable to crack down on rowdy ballplayers and managers. American League President Ban Johnson, however, dealt with the destructive forces of dirty play in summary fashion. In this report from the 1902 *Reach Guide,* we get a clear sense of his decisiveness—as well as his less-well-known ability to forgive.

From the very start President Johnson found it necessary to keep a firm rein on the imported National League managers and players who had been accustomed to doing pretty much as they pleased in the older organization, particularly in the matter of umpire-baiting.

Right at the start of the season some of the star players began to make things uncomfortable for President Johnson's umpire staff. . . . President Johnson had instructed these officials to promptly remove all kicking players from the game, regardless of consequence, and promised not only to stand by them at all times but to supplement their correction with further punishments when occasion demanded. And this policy President Johnson carried out vigorously. On May 20th he suspended Manager Duffy for ten days for abusing Umpire Manassau. In June Manager McGraw, of Baltimore, received a similar dose for repeated rows with umpires—an action which McGraw so bitterly resented that for several months he refused to speak to or hold any intercourse with the American League President.

On August 21st, at Baltimore, Pitcher McGinnity assaulted Umpire Connelly and spat in his face, for which he was expelled from the American League by President Johnson. The same day at Washington Pitcher Katoll threw a ball at Umpire Haskell, and Shortstop Shugart struck Haskell in the face. For this Katoll was suspended for the balance of the season, and Shugart, like McGinnity, was expelled from the American League. Later, however, President Johnson yielded to the strong petitions he was fairly deluged with and reinstated the players after suitable fines and apologies had been provided for.

Ty Cobb's classic slide. Boston pitcher Smoky Joe Wood: "Cobb always told me and other fellows he played against,
'All you've got to do is give me room to get in there and it'll be all right, but if you don't give me room, I'll cut my way in.'"

TY COBB: SLIDE SO IT HURTS

No player in the first quarter of this century inspired more respect, fear, and hatred than the Detroit Tigers' Ty Cobb. Nor has any ballplayer (except, perhaps, the Babe) ever gotten more ink. While early biographies spoke admiringly of his spunk and aggressive, clean play (one book was called *Ty Cobb, Idol of Baseball Fandom*), fans knew that Cobb was a cruel player who wanted so badly to succeed that his entire life was twisted by the effort. Even this excerpt from his mild, ghost-written 1914 autobiography, called *Busting 'Em and Other Big League Stories,* alludes to its subject's single-minded drive, a drive that culminated in a .367 lifetime batting average, 4191 hits, 892 stolen bases, and one of the first plaques in the Hall of Fame.

Cobb at bat in the 1907 World Series against the Chicago Cubs.

Opposite: "A player who can't fight is no good on a ball club," said Cobb—here, chatting with a police inspector assigned to protect him from angry opposing fans in 1915.

The great secret, to my mind, of being a good base runner is to hit the dirt with the feeling that you like the sensation. In the early months of a championship race, I am always covered with sliding blisters, as the pads are strapped fast to my legs under the uniform and slip when I do. But a player soon becomes toughened to these and has nothing toward the end of the season but some scars and callous spots. It is hardest to get going in the early weeks of the race when the sliding sores are bad, but even then a player must hit the dirt as if he enjoyed it.

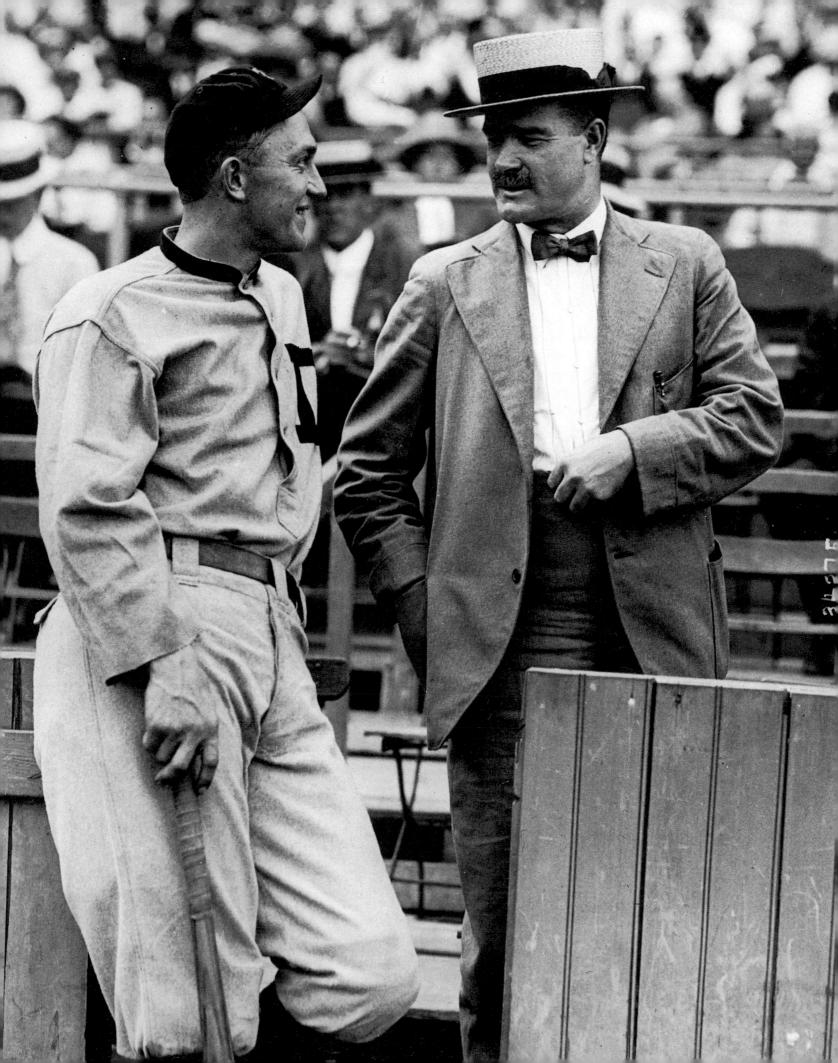

"WELL, HE WENT WILD"

This passage from Mickey Cochrane's *Baseball: The Fan's Game* (1939), detailing events from the Hall of Fame catcher's rookie year with Connie Mack's Philadelphia Athletics, vividly describes the fear-tinged respect that other players granted the great Ty Cobb, even late in his career.

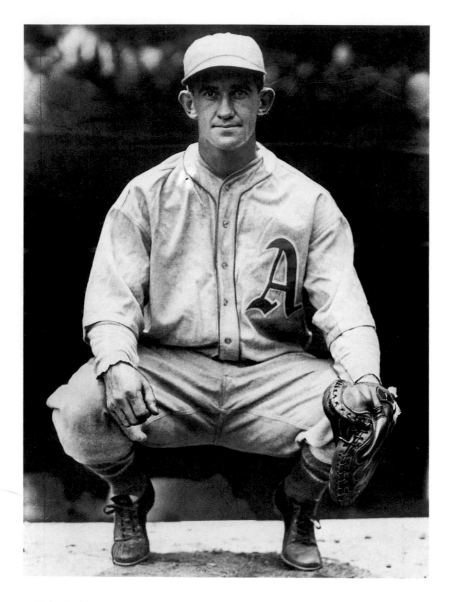

Mickey Cochrane, star catcher for the Philadelphia Athletics. Known as "Black Mike," Cochrane was a master of jockeying, an early version of trash talk.

That Athletics team of the old days, incidentally, was as ruthless and bitter a collection of jockeys as ever pulled on a spiked shoe. We formed a swashbuckling, arrogant, confident band of fellows—most of us rookies—in 1925, and we thought we were going to ride rough-shod over the league. And we were going through the motions of doing just that.

On a western trip we'd got on Cobb in a series in Detroit. Mr. Mack had warned us not to go to work on him, saying, "Leave that fellow Cobb alone, don't get him mad at you." But being young and foolish we thought the old gentleman, who'd been around since the league started, didn't know exactly what he was talking about.

We went into St. Louis for a series with the Browns, and for some reason or other commenced to turn our wrath and tongues on Ken Williams, a slugging outfielder, George Sisler, one of the finest gentlemen who ever played, and Marty McManus. Urban Shocker was pitching against us, and we went along all right in our swashbuckling way until the ninth inning of the first game. Sam Gray had a 3-to-1 lead, there were two out and two on, and Ken Williams at bat.

Gray was so cocky and confident that he selected the two-and-nothing ball as a place to try out a new pitch on which he had been working. Sam said this pitch would "sail" and he sailed it up to Williams who sailed it out of the park.

The Browns beat us 4–3. They beat us the next day, and in the last game of the series. What had been a five-and-a-half-game grasp on the first place was fast dissipating when we headed for Detroit. Remember, on our previous trip we rode Cobb, and he had told us in parting that he would knock us out of the pennant on the next trip around.

Well, he went wild. He got twelve hits in sixteen times at bat in a short series. He stole everything but the home plate and would have taken that except the series was being played in Detroit and he owned it anyway. He rode us unmercifully, fielded like a combination of Speaker, Hooper, Ruth and himself. He was in every argument, and in the beginning or payoff spot in every rally; in short, he had quite a time for himself.

Before we left town we were in second place, and before we could get hold of ourselves we lost thirteen straight. The swashbuckling arrogance of a bunch of fighting kids had contributed immensely to the slump which cost us the pennant. Our confidence could not stand up when the pressure got tight. The jockeying had paid dividends—for the opposition.

TRAVELS WITH HONUS

If Ty Cobb was baseball's dark presence, John Peter Wagner—better known, of course, as Honus or Hans—was his sunny counterpart. Beloved throughout a twenty-one-year major league career (1897–1917) spent mostly at shortstop with the Pittsburgh Pirates—during which he accumulated 722 stolen bases, 3418 hits, a .327 batting average, and a seat alongside Cobb in the first Hall of Fame class—Wagner spent years after his retirement as a Pirate coach. Here, in an interview with Pittsburgh publicity director Jim Long, relayed in a 1949 letter to Hall of Fame historian Ernest Lanigan, Wagner describes his peripatetic first professional season, including a little-known stint as a pitcher.

"In the National League he is a marked man," said Hall of Famer Johnny Evers of Honus Wagner (right and overleaf). "Yet, despite it all, he shines resplendent and continues to be the greatest of the great."

Dear Ernest:

It was not until today that I was able to corner Honus Wagner in order to get the dope you want about his first year out.

He recalls that he was with no fewer than six clubs during his first pro season, 1895, when he was just 21 years old. He started with Steubenville, O., in the Ohio State League, with his brother, Al, but he had not been there very long when the club and franchise were moved to Akron, O. After playing only three games in Akron, Wagner and his clubmates were shifted to Kent, O., and from that place they soon moved again, this time to Mansfield, O., in the Tri-State League.

Honus did so well while playing this base for Mansfield, that the chief owner, a man named Taylor, asked him if he would like to go Adrian, Mich., in the Michigan State League, to play for a club owned by his (Taylor's) brother, a hardware man.

When he arrived at Adrian, Honus was surprised to be informed by the Owner Taylor that he had been appointed manager. Wagner told the boss he had had no managerial experience, and that it was all new to him, but that he was game to take a crack at it. Honus says he found himself on a spot when all three of the regular pitchers reported that they would be unable to work on account of sore arms. There was no other course open to him than to go in and pitch himself, he relates. He got some help from outside by importing an independent Negro battery from a semi-pro club operated by the Page Fence Company. Their names were Johnson and Gray. Johnson pitched

Large and ungainly, Wagner possessed surprising speed, stealing 722 bases in his career and beating countless throws home.

and won the first game, Honus won the second, Johnson repeated in the third and Wagner was lucky enough to win again in the fourth. Honus was playing third base and shortstop between pitching appearances, and the club continued to have such success that at the end of three weeks it had risen to second place, and when the original three malingering pitchers asked to be taken back they were told their services were no longer desired. After playing in 20 games for Adrian, batting .365, Honus became homesick for Carnegie, and asked for and obtained his release. Later in that same 1895 season he joined the Warren (Pa.) Club, of the Iron and Oil League, batting .369 in 69 games.

1907: BIRTH OF A DOUBLE STANDARD

Honus Wagner may have played with black ballplayers in 1895, but by the turn of the century the color barrier had descended with frightening finality in the major and minor leagues. Still, for many years before Jackie Robinson entered the National League in 1947, white ballplayers (including such superstars as Babe Ruth) competed against Josh Gibson, Satchel Paige, and other Negro League stars, playing sold-out exhibition games during the off-season. But barnstorming began far earlier and more modestly. As Sol White points out in the little-known *History of Colored Base-Ball During 1907,* white and black ballplayers played against each other in the early 1900s—and then, as always, the black players held their own.

Sol White (center), Rube Foster (third from left), and other players of the Royal Poinciana Hotel, Palm Beach, Florida, in 1905.

Palm Beach, Fla., has been the Mecca for colored ball players during the Winter seasons. The two large hotels there giving them employment and the beautiful base ball grounds near the Royal Poinciana, the largest hotel in the World, affords them the opportunity of making a neat sum of money through the games played between teams representing the Poinciana and the Breakers hotels.

F. Allen and Wm. Evans have been the headwaiters to promote base ball at this great Winter resort.

A. M. Thompson, now headwaiter of the Royal Palm Hotel, Miami, Fla., has entered the field and will place a fast colored team in Miami to represent the Royal Palm.

Seabreeze and Ormond are represented by white teams composed of American and National League players, and the contests between the colored boys of Palm Beach and the white boys from Ormond and Seabreeze are looked for yearly and draw immense crowds. Such players as Delehanty, McIntyre, Applegate and Wakefield of the American League; Ritchie, Needham and Dugan of the National League, play with Ormond and Seabreeze.

Of the four games played between the white and colored teams last Winter, the white boys failed to win a game.

1908: THE MOST FAMOUS PENNANT RACE OF ALL

Even more than eighty-five years later, the extraordinary 1908 National League race—featuring such great personalities as Hall of Famers Christy Mathewson, John McGraw, and Three Finger Brown, and such spectacles as Fred Merkle's infamous "boner" and the riotous Cubs-Giants playoff game for the National League championship—remains vivid in our minds. Though memorialized in Lawrence Ritter's *The Glory of Their Times* (1966), in G. H. Fleming's *The Unforgettable Season* (1981), and in countless other baseball histories, perhaps the most exciting depictions of that great race come from two key participants: Mathewson and Johnny "the Crab" Evers, the Cubs' Hall of Fame second baseman.

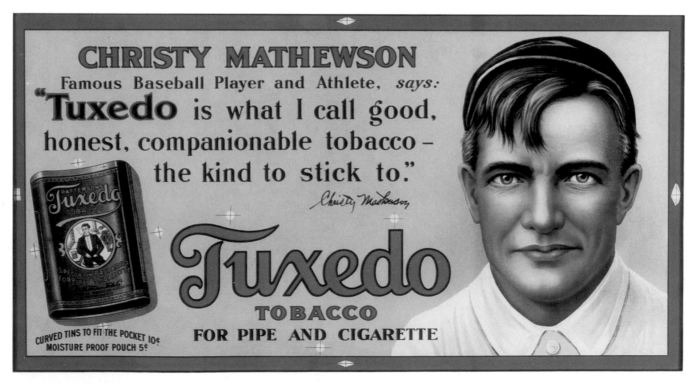

Christy Mathewson: A famous face in early 1900s baseball.

Johnny "the Crab" Evers: High-strung, hard to get along with—and always willing to tell the umpires what was what.

The Man Behind Merkle's Boner

In *My Greatest Day in Baseball* (1945), Evers told writer John P. Carmichael about the day Merkle committed his irretrievable and notorious mistake.

It is 36 years now since the day Fred Merkle didn't touch second, but it could be 135 and I'd never forget what happened. I can't get around much any more with this bum leg, so sitting in this chair day after day there's nothing much to do but live in the past. You know most of the stories afterward said Umpire Hank O'Day walked off the field without saying a word as the fans came down on the diamond under the impression New York had won 2–1. But he didn't. He stayed right there and waited for me to make the play and told me the Giant run didn't count.

The Merkle affair occurred Sept. 23, 1908, but it was 19 days earlier, at Pittsburgh, that we really won the game at New York. The same play came up against the Pirates and O'Day was the umpire then too. Mordecai Brown was pitching for the Cubs and he'd shut out the Bucs three straight times earlier in the season. This day they hadn't scored off him again in nine innings, making it 36 frames he'd held them runless, but we couldn't get anything off Vic Willis either. In the 10th we got beat.

Fred Clarke was on third, Wagner on second and Gill on first with Wilson at the plate. Wilson singled to center and Jimmy Slagle threw the ball back to the infield as Clarke, of course, went on home. But Gill didn't go to second. He ran off the field. I got the ball and hollered to O'Day to look. He wouldn't. I stood on second and yelled

Johnny Evers (right) and Joe Tinker (opposite), two-thirds of the most famous double-play combination of all time—and pivotal figures in the Cubs' sensational pennant victory.

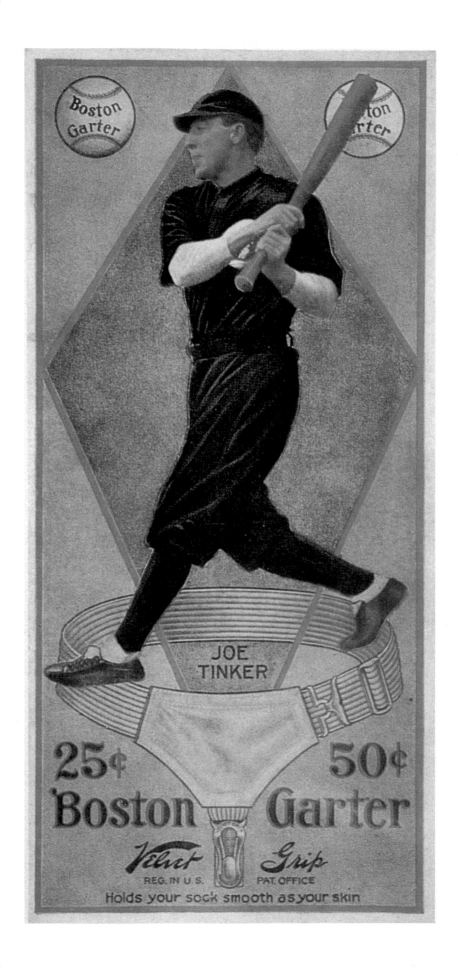

*Fiery John J. McGraw and cool
Christy Mathewson, partners in
victory and demoralizing defeat.*

that the run didn't count . . . that Gill was the third out, but Hank refused to listen.
"Clarke scored before the out could have been made," he told Manager Frank Chance
and pushed his way to the dressing room.

Ol' Hank was mad at me anyway for an argument we'd had in St. Louis a few
weeks before and you could tell that his whole attitude was he'd be damned if that little
squirt Evers was going to get him in another jam. But just the same he was a good
umpire . . . if you didn't tell him so too often . . . and he realized later what had
happened and in the long run we got the break when we needed it most in New York.
As everybody knows, we couldn't have won the pennant if we hadn't.

There were only about 10 points between the Giants and us by Sept. 23. This was the last game of the series and McGraw sent Christy Mathewson to the mound. Jack Pfiester was pitching for us. O'Day and Bob Emslie were the umpires and there were 25,000 fans there easily. In the fifth inning we got in front when Joe Tinker hit a home run. It really was just a line drive to the outfield but Donlin tried to make a shoestring catch and the ball rolled past him and Joe got all the way around. In the next inning the Giants tied it as Herzog beat out a slow roller to Steinfeldt at third and got to second when Harry made a bad throw to first. Up came Donlin and squared himself for missing Tinker's ball with a single that scored Herzog.

So that's the way we stood going into the ninth and to show you what a pitcher's battle it was, Tinker handled 14 chances that game and I had 11 which was as many as I had in any game all season. Matty set us down one-two-three in our half and New York put on a rally. With one out, Devlin singled and McCormick slashed one right at me. It was just slow enough so the best Tinker and I could do was to get Devlin at second. Still there were two gone even if McCormick was safe. Up came Merkle. He was just a rookie at that time and probably wouldn't have been playing if we hadn't had a southpaw working, but McGraw wanted to get as much right-handed hitting into his lineup as possible and anyway Fred Tenney had a bum ankle and could use extra rest, so Merkle was at first.

New York Giants first baseman Fred Merkle, never to be forgotten for what The New York Times *called his "censurable stupidity."*

Well, he singled and McCormick went to third. Al Bridwell was the next hitter and he singled to center. That's where the fun began.

Artie Hofman threw the ball in as McCormick went home and Merkle jogged halfway to second. I had my eye on him, saw him stop, glance around at the fans pouring out of their seats, and start for the clubhouse beyond right field. Hofman's throw had gone over Tinker's head and rolled over to where Joe McGinnity, the Giant pitcher, was standing. Joe'd been coaching on third and he knew what was in our minds as Tinker and I raced for the ball. He got it first, but before he could get rid of the thing, Joe and I had him and we wrestled around there for what seemed to be five minutes. Of course it wasn't.

We grabbed for his hands to make sure he wouldn't heave the ball away but he broke loose and tossed it into the crowd. I can see the fellow who caught it yet . . . a tall, stringy middle-aged gent with a brown bowler hat on. Steinfeldt and Floyd Kroh, a young pitcher we'd added to our staff during the summer, raced after him. "Gimme the ball for just a minute," Steinfeldt begged him. "I'll bring it right back." The guy wouldn't let go and suddenly Kroh solved the problem. He hit the customer right on top of that stiff hat, drove it down over his eyes and as the gent folded up, the ball fell free and Kroh got it. I was yelling and waving my hands out by second base and Tinker relayed it over to me and I stepped on the bag and made sure O'Day saw me. As I said before, he was waiting for that very play . . . he remembered the Pittsburgh game . . . and he said: "The run does not count." Then he walked away. But he made no attempt to continue the game in the confusion.

There was hell a-poppin' after that. Emslie refused to take a stand for or against O'Day. "I didn't see the play," he insisted and that's all he'd say. Mathewson and a couple of the Giants dashed for the clubhouse and tried to get Merkle back to second, but I was standing there with the ball before they got him out the door. They saw it was too late, although McGraw kept hollering that the Giants had won and the fans, who only knew the Cubs were trying to pull off some trick, gave us a good going over. A couple of park "fly cops" which McGraw had scattered around to "protect" the visiting players took a few pokes at Chance under the guise of keeping the crowd back and there must have been five fist fights going on as we finally got out of there.

But at least we won the game, eventually . . . that is we played it off Oct. 8 and Brown won, 4–2. President Harry Pulliam of the league backed O'Day in his decision, but the Giants protested so vigorously and long that the board of directors finally had to settle matters. I'm not so sure they would have decided in our favor at that, but Jack Ryder, the old Cincinnati writer, who is dead now, broke into the meeting and delivered a helluva speech in our favor, claiming there was no choice but to play the game over and vowing that the league would make itself a laughingstock if it let the Giants get away with a pennant on a bonehead play.

So it turned out all right for us, but one day during the off-season I ran into Roger Bresnahan, who caught Matty that afternoon, and the Giant catcher showed me a medal. It was one of 28 which John T. Brush, Giant owner, had struck off for each member of the team and showed a ballplayer with a bat in his hand and another throwing a ball and the inscription read:

"The Real Champions, 1908."

*"All the Thrills of the Diamond,"
but none of the heartbreak
Christy experienced on the real
playing field.*

"The Most Dramatic and Important Contest in the History of Baseball"

Partly as a result of O'Day's decision, the Cubs and the Giants finished the season with identical records of 98–55, which required them to play the first playoff game in league history. Christy Mathewson's *Pitching in a Pinch* (1912), written with John N. Wheeler, captures all the excitement and tension of that memorable afternoon.

The New York Giants and the Chicago Cubs played a game at the Polo Grounds on October 8, 1908, which decided the championship of the National League in one afternoon, which was responsible for the deaths of two spectators, who fell from the elevated railroad structure overlooking the grounds, which made Fred Merkle famous

"When I pitched that extra play-off game against the Cubs," Mathewson told writer Grantland Rice, "my arm was so sore and stiff I needed an hour's warm-up. I could barely lift it."

for not touching second, which caused lifelong friends to become bitter enemies, and which, altogether, was the most dramatic and important contest in the history of baseball. It stands out from every-day events like the battle of Waterloo and the assassination of President Lincoln. It was a baseball tragedy from a New York point of view. The Cubs won by the score of 4 to 2. . . .

That night was a wild one in New York. The air crackled with excitement and baseball. I went home, but couldn't sleep for I live near the Polo Grounds, and the crowd began to gather there early in the evening of the day before the game to be ready for the opening of the gates the next morning. They tooted horns all night, and were never still. When I reported at the ball park, the gates had been closed by order of the National Commission, but the streets for blocks around the Polo Grounds were jammed with persons fighting to get to the entrances.

The players in the clubhouse had little to say to one another, but, after the bandages were adjusted, McGraw called his men around him and said:

"Chance will probably pitch Pfiester or Brown. If Pfiester works there is no use trying to steal. He won't give you any lead. The right-handed batters ought to wait him out and the left-handers hit him when he gets in a hole. Matty is going to pitch for us."

Pfiester is a left-hand pitcher who watches the bases closely.

Merkle had reported at the clubhouse as usual and had put on his uniform. He hung on the edge of the group as McGraw spoke, and then we all went to the field. It was hard for us to play that game with the crowd which was there, but harder for the Cubs. In one place, the fence was broken down, and some employees were playing a stream of water from a fire hose on the cavity to keep the crowd back. Many preferred a ducking to missing the game and ran through the stream to the lines around the field. A string of fans recklessly straddled the roof of the old grand-stand.

Every once in a while some group would break through the restraining ropes and scurry across the diamond to what appeared to be a better point of vantage. This would let a throng loose which hurried one way and another and mixed in with the players. More police had to be summoned. As I watched that half-wild multitude before the contest, I could think of three or four things I would rather do than umpire the game.

I had rested my arm four days, not having pitched in a Boston series, and I felt that it should be in pretty good condition. Before that respite, I had been in nine out of fifteen games. But as I started to warm up, the ball refused to break. I couldn't get anything on it.

"What's the matter, Rog?" I asked Bresnahan. "They won't break for me."

"It'll come as you start to work," he replied, although I could see that he, too, was worried.

John M. Ward, the old ball-player and now one of the owners of the Boston National League club, has told me since that, after working almost every day as I had been doing, it does a pitcher's arm no good to lay off for three or four days. Only a week or ten days will accomplish any results. It would have been better for me to continue to work as often as I had been doing, for the short rest only seemed to deaden my arm.

The crowd that day was inflammable. The players caught this incendiary spirit. McGinnity, batting out to our infield in practice, insisted on driving Chance away from the plate before the Cubs' leader thought his team had had its full share of the batting rehearsal. "Joe" shoved him a little, and in a minute fists were flying, although Chance and McGinnity are very good friends off the field.

Fights immediately started all around in the stands. I remember seeing two men roll from the top to the bottom of the right-field bleachers, over the heads of the rest of the spectators. And they were yanked to their feet and run out of the park by the police.

"Too bad," I said to Bresnahan, nodding my head toward the departing belligerents, "they couldn't have waited until they saw the game, anyway. I'll bet they stood outside the park all night to get in, only to be run out before it started."

I forgot the crowd, forgot the fights, and didn't hear the howling after the game started. I knew only one thing, and that was my curved ball wouldn't break for me. It surprised me that the Cubs didn't hit it far, right away, but two of them fanned in the first inning and Herzog threw out Evers. Then came our first time at bat. Pfiester was plainly nervous and hit Tenney. Herzog walked and Bresnahan fanned out, Herzog being doubled up at second because he tried to advance on a short passed ball. "Mike" Donlin whisked a double to right field and Tenney counted.

For the first time . . . Merkle smiled. He was drawn up in the corner of the bench, pulling away from the rest of us as if he had some contagious disease and was quarantined. For a minute it looked as if we had them going. Chance yanked Pfiester out of the box with him protesting that he had been robbed on the decisions on balls and strikes. Brown was brought into the game and fanned Devlin. That ended the inning.

We never had a chance against Brown. His curve was breaking sharply, and his control was microscopic. We went back to the field in the second with that one run lead. Chance made the first hit of the game off me in the second, but I caught him sleeping at first base, according to Klem's decision. There was a kick, and Hofman, joining in the chorus of protests, was sent to the clubhouse.

Tinker started the third with that memorable triple which gave the Cubs their chance. I couldn't make my curve break. I didn't have anything on the ball.

"Rog," I said to Bresnahan, "I haven't got anything to-day."

"Keep at it, Matty," he replied. "We'll get them all right."

I looked in at the bench, and McGraw signalled me to go on pitching. Kling singled and scored Tinker. Brown sacrificed, sending Kling to second, and Sheckard flied out to Seymour, Kling being held on second base. I lost Evers, because I was afraid to put the ball over the plate for him, and he walked. Two were out now, and we had yet a chance to win the game as the score was only tied. But Schulte doubled, and Kling scored, leaving men on second and third bases. Still we had a Mongolian's chance with them only one run ahead of us. Frank Chance, with his under jaw set like the fender on a trolley car, caught a curved ball over the inside corner of the plate and pushed it to right field for two bases. That was the most remarkable batting performance I have ever witnessed since I have been in the Big Leagues. A right-handed hitter naturally slaps a ball over the outside edge of the plate to right field, but Chance pushed this one, on the inside, with the handle of his bat, just over Tenney's hands and on into the crowd. The hit scored Evers and Schulte and dissolved the game right there. It was the "break." Steinfeldt fanned.

None of the players spoke to one another as they went to the bench. Even McGraw was silent. We knew it was gone. Merkle was drawn up behind the water cooler. Once he said:

"It was my fault, boys."

No one answered him. Inning after inning, our batters were mowed down by the great pitching of Brown, who was never better. His control of his curved ball was marvellous, and he had all his speed. As the innings dragged by, the spectators lost heart, and the cowbells ceased to jingle, and the cheering lost its resonant ring. It was now a surly growl.

Then the seventh! We had our one glimmer of sunshine. Devlin started with a single to centre, and McCormick shoved a drive to right field. Recalling that Bridwell was more or less of a pinch hitter, Brown passed him purposely and Doyle was sent to the bat in my place. As he hobbled to the plate on his weak foot, said McGraw:

"Hit one, Larry."

Mordecai "Three Finger" Brown, who attributed his unhittable curve and great control to the accident that amputated part of his pitching hand.

The crowd broke into cheers again and was stamping its feet. The bases were full, and no one was out. Then Doyle popped up a weak foul behind the catcher. His batting eye was dim and rusty through long disuse. Kling went back for it, and some one threw a pop bottle which narrowly missed him, and another scaled a cushion. But Kling kept on and got what he went after, which was the ball. He has a habit of doing that. Tenney flied to Schulte, counting Devlin on the catch, and Tinker threw out Herzog. The game was gone. Never again did we have a chance.

It was a glum lot of players in the clubhouse. Merkle came up to McGraw and said:

"Mac, I've lost you one pennant. Fire me before I can do any more harm."

"Fire you?" replied McGraw. "We ran the wrong way of the track to-day. That's all. Next year is another season, and do you think I'm going to let you go after the gameness you've shown through all this abuse? Why you're the kind of guy I've been lookin' for many years. I could use a carload like you. Forget this season and come around next spring. The newspapers will have forgotten it all then. Good-by, boys." And he slipped out of the clubhouse.

"He's a regular guy," said Merkle.

Merkle has lived down that failure to touch second and proved himself to be one of the gamest players that ever stood in a diamond. Many times since has he vindicated himself. He is a great first baseman now, and McGraw and he are close friends. That is the "inside" story of the most important game ever played in baseball and Merkle's connection with it.

"WILLIE'S BROTHER'S DEMISE"

From "Jack" Regan and Will E. Stahl, *Around the World with the Baseball Bugs* (1910)

Willie was an office boy,
    Willie was a fan;
Willie knew more about baseball
    Than many an older man.
Willie said his brother
    Was sick as a man could be
And "Please could he get off to-day
    To bear him companee?"

"You may," the Boss said, gently,
    Gazing at Willie the while
And Willie's look as he stood there
    Was totally free from guile.
His head bowed low with sorrow,
    He slowly went outside
While gloom hung over the office.
    And the secretary cried.

Next day he showed up at the office,
    With a frown as black as night;
The Boss, with kindly manner,
    Inquired if all was not right.
"Not on your life," said Willie,
    Forgetting himself in his rage,
Which was rather improper of Willie,
    Considering he wasn't of age.

"Oh tell me, Willie, tell me,"
    The gentle Boss then cried;
"Your brother—is he safe at home?
    Or has the poor chap died?"
"I should say he wasn't safe at home
    (There was venom in every word),
"In the end of the ninth—de score a tie—
    The sucker DIED AT THIRD!"

BOSTON-AMERICAN LEAGUE CHAMPIONS—1912

MANAGER STAHL · 1912 · CAPTAIN WAGNER · PRESIDENT McALEER

O'BRIEN · CARRIGAN C · WOOD P · NUNAMAKER C · SPEAKER C.F. · HENRIKSON R.F. · HALL P · CICOTTE P · GARDNER 3d B. · WAGNER S.S. · THOMAS C · HOOPER R.F. · LEWIS L.F. · HAGERMAN P · LEONARD P · Dr. QUIRK · PAPE P · ENGLE U · YERKES 2d B. · BRADLEY 1st B. · KRUG S.S. · BEDIENT P · BUSHELMAN P · CADY C · McCARTHY Mascot · STAHL 1st B.

1912: CHRISTY'S HEARTBREAK, PART TWO

The 1912 World Series, one of the most exciting of all time, pitted John McGraw and Christy Mathewson's New York Giants against Jake Stahl's Boston Red Sox, starring Tris Speaker and Smoky Joe Wood, who had gone 34–5 with an ERA of 1.91 during the regular season. The series was tied after seven games. (Game Two was a tie.) The Giants, with Mathewson pitching, took a 2–1 lead in the top of the tenth inning of the eighth game. But then, in the bottom of the tenth, came perhaps the most famous error of all time: Fred Snodgrass's muff of a catchable fly ball, which helped the Sox mount a two-run, game-winning rally. As in 1908, fate had dealt a bum hand to John McGraw. ("The bitter, enraged expression that settled on his thick face in his last years," Roger Angell writes of McGraw, "was the look of a man who had fought a lifelong, bareknuckled fight against bad baseball luck.") And once again Christy Mathewson, one of the greatest pitchers in baseball history, had lost a crucial game he was close—so close—to winning.

"Tears Rolled Down His Sun-Burned Cheeks"
From T. H. Murnane, *The Boston Globe* (October 17, 1912)

Words were never invented that could fully describe the outburst of insane enthusiasm that went thundering around Fenway Park yesterday afternoon as Steve Yerkes crossed the rubber with the winning run in the 10th inning.

Men hugged each other, women became hysterical, youths threw their caps in the air, one man in the bleachers fell in a dead faint, strong hearts lost a beat and started off again at double time.

John McGraw, the little Napoleon, dashed across the field to offer his congratulations to Manager Jake Stahl. The cheering lasted fully five minutes, while the Boston players, all smiles, modestly retired to their dressing rooms.

The great New York fighting machine had lost at the last ditch, and with heads bowed low the Giants pushed through the crowd, practically unnoticed.

Christy Mathewson, the greatest pitcher of all time, had lost, after pitching a remarkable game. It was no fault of his. It was the one game in his 12 years on the ball field that he had set his heart on winning, for it meant the championship of the world and one more thrill before passing out of the limelight as a remarkable performer.

Mathewson, the baseball genius, was heartbroken and tears rolled down his sun-burned cheeks as he was consoled by his fellow-players.

In its frenzy the crowd could only see the victors, and yet the defeated National League champions were no less worthy of appreciation, considering the game fight they put up from first to last in the most remarkable series of games ever played.

Giants' catcher Chief Meyers beats Red Sox slugger Tris Speaker to first base in this rare action shot from the 1912 World Series.

Mathewson's Cunning Was Not Enough
From John Buckingham Foster, *Spalding Guide* (1913)

No individual, whether player, manager, owner, critic or spectator, who went through the world's series of 1912 ever will forget it. There never was another like it. Years may elapse before there shall be a similar series and it may be that the next to come will be equally sensational, perhaps more so.

Viewed from the very strict standpoint that all Base Ball games should be played without mistake or blunder this world's series may be said to have been inartistic, but it is only the hypercritical theorist who would take such a cold-blooded view of the series.

From the lofty perch of the "bleacherite" it was a series crammed with thrills and gulps, cheers and gasps, pity and hysteria, dejection and wild exultation, recrimination and adoration, excuse and condemnation, and therefore it was what may cheerfully be called "ripping good" Base Ball.

There were plays on the field which simply lifted the spectators out of their seats in frenzy. There were others which caused them to wish to sink through the hard floor of the stand in humiliation. There were stops in which fielders seemed to stretch like india rubber and others in which they shriveled like parchment which has been dried. There were catches of fly balls which were superhuman and muffs of fly balls which were "superawful."

There were beautiful long hits, which threatened to change the outcome of games and some of them did. There were opportunities for other beautiful long hits which were not made.

No ingenuity of stage preparation, no prearranged plot of man, no cunningly devised theory of a world's series could have originated a finale equal to that of the eighth and decisive contest. Apparently on the verge of losing the series after the Saturday game in Boston the Giants had gamely fought their way to a tie with Boston, and it was one of the pluckiest and gamest fights ever seen in a similar series, and just as the golden apple seemed about to drop into the hands of the New York players they missed it because Dame Fortune rudely jostled them aside.

Fred Snodgrass, whose famous "muff" of a catchable fly ball contributed to a World Series loss for the Giants.

As a matter of fact the New York players were champions of the world for nine and one half innings, for they led Boston when the first half of the extra inning of the final game was played. Within the next six minutes they had lost all the advantage which they had gained.

It was a combination of bad fielding and lack of fielding which cost the New York team its title. And if only Mathewson had not given Yerkes a base on balls in the tenth inning the game might not have been won, even with the fielding blunders, but Mathewson was pitching with all the desperation and the cunning which he could muster to fool the batter and failed to do so.

Such sudden and complete reversal on the part of the mental demeanor of spectators was never before seen on a ball field in a world's series. The Boston enthusiasts had given up and were willing to concede the championship to New York. In the twinkling of an eye there was a muffed fly, a wonderful catch by the same player who muffed the ball—Snodgrass—a base on balls to Yerkes, a missed chance to retire Speaker easily on a foul fly, then a base hit by Speaker to right field, on which Engel scored, another base on balls to Lewis and then the long sacrifice fly to right field by Gardner, which sent Yerkes over the plate with the winning run.

Smoky Joe Wood, who went 34–5 and led the Red Sox to the 1912 World Championship.

"Manhattan vs. Smoky Joe"
From *The Boston Globe* (October 11, 1912)

Of all sad words from tongue or pen
The saddest are "Wood pitched again";
Sadder than any throbbing note
That old Doc Chopin ever wrote;
Aye, sadder in its sombre skit
Than life's worst message—"Please remit."

Wood Pitched Again—tell me no more
The ultimate—the final score;
Waste no vain words in praise or blame,

Explaining which side copped the game;
Who blew the works—who had the stuff—
Wood Pitched—that's bally well enough.

Wood Pitched Again—O bitter phrase—
O blighting echo of the days;
Sadder than any New York cop,
Or "Could you slip me five, old top?"
Aye, in each dreary Harlem flat
Sadder than "Baker at the bat."

O Death, where is thy sting like this?
O Grave, where is thy serpent's kiss?
O Baker, Bender, Coombs and Plank,
You look like money in the bank,
Compared to this last scratch of pen—
"Wood pitched again."

Walter Johnson.

TWO VIEWS OF THE BIG TRAIN

Widely thought to throw harder than any other pitcher of his time, Walter Johnson (known as the Big Train) concluded a twenty-one-year career with the Washington Senators with an extraordinary 416 wins and a lifetime ERA of 2.17. Even as a nineteen year old he was something special, as Hall of Fame pitcher Addie Joss saw midway through 1907, Johnson's rookie year. But, as George Sisler, a Hall of Fame first baseman who also pitched early in his career with the St. Louis Browns, discovered in 1915 (when Johnson went 27–13, with an ERA of 1.55), even the Big Train in his prime wasn't unbeatable.

Addie Joss Could Spot 'Em
From *Sporting Life* (August 24, 1907)

Addie Joss said of young Johnson, the new Washington pitching find: "That young fellow is another Cy Young. I never saw a kid with more than he displayed. Of course, he is still green, but when he has a little experience he should be one of the greatest pitchers that ever broke into the game. He has terrific speed and a motion which does not put much strain on his arm. And this will all improve as he goes along."

Even Heroes Fall
From George Sisler, as told to Lyall Smith, *My Greatest Day in Baseball* (1945)

Every American kid has a baseball idol. Mine was Walter Johnson, the "Big Train." Come to think about it, Walter still is my idea of the real baseball player. He was graceful. He had rhythm and when he heaved that ball in to the plate he threw with his whole body just so easy-like that you'd think the ball was flowing off his arm and hand.

"I don't think there ever was a pitcher in Walter Johnson's class," said Smoky Joe Wood.

I was just a husky kid in Akron (Ohio) High School back around 1910–11 when Johnson began making a name for himself with the Senators and I was so crazy about the man that I'd read every line and keep every picture of him I could get my hands on.

Naturally, admiring Johnson as I did, I decided to be a pitcher and even though I wound up as a first baseman my biggest day in baseball was a hot muggy afternoon in St. Louis when I pitched against him and beat him. Never knew that, did you? Most fans don't. But it's right. Me, a kid just out of the University of Michigan beat the great Walter Johnson. It was on August 29, 1915, my first year as a baseball player, the first time I ever was in a game against the man who I thought was the greatest pitcher in the world. . . .

After the Saturday game [manager Branch] Rickey stuck his head in the locker room and told me I was going to pitch against Johnson the next day. I went back to my hotel that night but I couldn't eat. I was really nervous. I went to bed but I couldn't sleep. At 4:00 A.M. I was tossing and rolling around and finally got up and just sat there, waiting for daylight and the big game.

I managed to stick it out, got some breakfast in me and was out at Sportsman's Park before the gates opened. It was one of those typical August days in St. Louis and when game time finally rolled around it was so hot that the sweat ran down your face even when you were standing in the shadow of the stands.

All the time I was warming up I'd steal a look over at Johnson in the Washington bull pen. When he'd stretch 'way out and throw in a fast ball I'd try to do the same thing. Even when I went over to the dugout just before the game started I was still watching him as he signed autographs and laughed with the photographers and writers.

Well, the game finally started and I tried to be calm. First man to face me was Moeller, Washington's left fielder. I didn't waste any time and stuck three fast ones in there to strike him out. Eddie Foster was up next and he singled to right field. Charley Milan singled to right center and I was really scared. I could see Mr. Rickey leaning out of the dugout watching me real close so I kept them high to Shanks and got him to fly out to Walker in center field. He hit it back pretty far though and Foster, a fast man, started out for third base. Walker made a perfect peg into the infield but Johnny Lavan, our shortstop, fumbled the relay and Foster kept right on going to score. That was all they got in that inning, but I wasn't feeling too sure when I came in to the bench. I figured we weren't going to get many runs off Johnson and I knew I couldn't be giving up many runs myself.

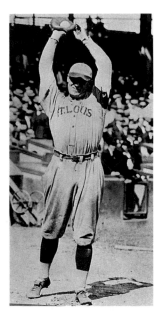

George Sisler needed skill—and lots of luck—to beat the Big Train.

Then Johnson went out to face us and I really got a thrill out of watching him pitch. He struck out the first two Brownies and made Del Pratt fly to short center. Then I had to go out again and I got by all right. In the second inning, Walker led off with a single to center field and Baby Doll Jacobson dumped a bunt in front of the plate. Otto Williams, Washington catcher, scooped it up and threw it 10 feet over the first baseman's head. Walker already was around second and he came in and scored while the Baby Doll reached third.

I think I actually felt sorry for Johnson. I knew just how he felt because after all, the same thing had happened to me in the first inning. Del Howard was next up for us and he singled Jacobson home to give us two runs and give me a 2–1 lead.

Well, that was all the scoring for the day, although I gave up five more hits over the route. Johnson got one in the first of the fifth, a blooper over second. I was up in the last of the same inning and I'll be darned if I didn't get the same kind. So he and I were even up anyway. We each hit one man, too.

There wasn't much more to the game. Only one man reached third on me after the first inning and only two got that far on Johnson.

When I got the last man out in the first of the ninth and went off the field I looked down at the Washington bench hoping to get another look at Johnson. But he already had ducked down to the locker room.

I don't know what I expected to do if I had seen him. For a minute I thought maybe I'd go over and shake his hand and tell him that I was sorry I beat him but I guess that was just a silly idea of a young kid who had just come face to face with his idol and beaten him.

1920: A DEATH ON THE FIELD

One of the two calamities that stunned the baseball world in 1920 was the death of popular Cleveland shortstop Ray Chapman on August 17, killed by a pitch thrown by submariner Carl Mays. The following excerpts paint a stark portrait of the daily fear confronted by batters facing fastball pitchers such as Mays and Walter Johnson, as well as the events that occurred on August 17 and some of the consequences of Chapman's death.

Even Cobb Was Afraid
From F. C. Lane, *Batting* (1925)

Not only pitchers are afraid of being beaned, the greatest batters sometimes have the same fear. Ty Cobb said, "Walter Johnson, for a long time, had me buffaloed. I wouldn't admit it to anyone else, and I don't think I ever showed it. But I had a dread amounting almost to positive fear of his fast ball. I have a vivid recollection of how it seemed to me when I faced Walter. That accursed fast ball of his used to whistle when it shot past. I found myself unconsciously speculating on just what would happen if that ball hit me on the head. It wasn't a pretty picture."

The Death of Ray Chapman
From Fred Lieb, *Baseball As I Have Known It* (1978)

"Doctoring the ball is cheap business," opined The Sporting News *in 1919. "It has no place in America's greatest and cleanest pastime." Opposite: Ray Chapman, whose death the next year led baseball officials to ban the spitball and other "freak" pitches.*

The weather was hot and sultry in the Polo Grounds that afternoon. Two clubs which had never won an American League pennant, the Cleveland Indians and the New York Yankees, were battling for their first championship. Both managers, Miller Huggins and Tris Speaker, had started their best pitchers, Carl Mays and Stan Coveleski, a spitballer who in a decade (1916–25) won 193 games. Mays was unsteady in the early innings, and the Indians led, 3–0, when Mays faced Ray Chapman, star shortstop, Cleveland's first hitter in the top of the fifth inning.

With a count of one strike and one ball on the batter, Mays let go a pitch with results that would haunt him for the rest of his life. It was high on the inside, designed to prevent Chapman from attempting a drag bunt, one of Ray's specialties. Sitting in the old downstairs press box, not much more than fifty feet behind the umpire, I had a perfect view of the action. A right-handed hitter, Chapman crouched over the plate more than any other batter of his era. I saw Mays's "submarine" pitch rise, from the near-ground level where it was delivered, on a straight line towards Chapman's head. A batter has about a half second to react to a ball that may hit him. As soon as Ray was hit I thought, "Why didn't he react, duck, throw himself to the ground?" But he didn't. He froze.

There was a sickening thud as the ball hit the left side of Chapman's head at the temple. He got up after a few seconds, and I could see the left eye hanging from its socket. With a ball player's instinct, he took two steps toward first, then fell in a heap. He never regained consciousness. Cleveland players carried him to the center-field clubhouse, and from there he was rushed to a downtown hospital. He died at 3:30 A.M. the next morning, the only big leaguer to be a fatal victim of a pitched ball.

Carl Mays' Defense
From F. C. Lane, *Batting* (1925)

What added to the tragedy was the maze of rumor and criticism which sought to hold Mays responsible for the affair. Mays himself explained his part in the proceeding. He said, "The death of Ray Chapman is a thing I do not like to discuss. It is an episode

that I shall always regret more than anything else that ever happened to me. And yet, I can look into my own conscience and feel absolved from all sense of guilt. The most amazing thing about it was the fact that some people seemed to believe I did this thing deliberately. Now I am a pitcher and I know some of the things a pitcher can do and some he cannot do. I know that a pitcher cannot stand on the slab, sixty feet from the plate, and throw a baseball so that he can hit a batter in the head, once in a hundred times. But to kill a man it is not enough even to hit him on the head. Walter Johnson, with all his terrific speed, has hit batters on the head and yet they did not die. There is only one spot on a player's skull where a pitched ball would do him fatal injury. That is a spot about his temple which isn't half as large as the palm of my hand. Suppose a pitcher were moral monster enough to want to kill a batter with whom he can have no possible quarrel. How could he do this terrible thing? Christy Mathewson in the days of his most perfect control couldn't have hit a batter in the temple once in a thousand tries."

Batting Helmets, An Idea Whose Time Had Not Come
From *The New York Times* (August 19, 1920)

Headgear for ball players, to use while batting, is being considered by club owners and players as a result of the unfortunate accident which resulted in the death of Ray Chapman this week and it will not be surprising if batsmen of the future go to the plate with a covering on that side of the head that is nearest to the opposing pitcher.

That club officials had the subject under consideration was disclosed yesterday by Magistrate F. X. McQuade, Treasurer of the Giants. When asked if the headgear would

A 1930s batting helmet. Despite Ray Chapman's death and other serious beanings, major league players resisted using helmets until the 1950s.

Opposite: Carl Mays' submarine delivery, which froze Ray Chapman—and helped change the future of baseball.

resemble the helmets such as are sometimes used by aviators and which were quite the vogue in football in former years, he declared that nothing definite had been decided upon. It is probable, however, that sporting goods manufacturers will offer some models and the one which seems to suit conditions the best will be adopted.

Though the idea of headgear in baseball will sound strange to the fans, the adoption of such a form of protection will be following the trend of the sport to bring out at intervals protective devices that lessen the tendency to injury on the part of the player. When introduced the various devices invariably met with some ridicule on the part of players who had gone through years of service without the protecting equipment, and from the fans as well, but in turn each additional bit of armor has come to be regarded as an essential.

Eddie Cicotte, whose role in throwing the 1919 Series derailed what would likely have been a Hall of Fame career.

*Joe Jackson out by a mile stealing, Game One. Watching Jackson and the other White Sox play, writer
Ring Lardner began to sing "I'm Forever Throwing Ballgames" to the popular tune of "I'm Forever Blowing Bubbles."*

THE BLACK SOX: ANATOMY OF A SCANDAL

No episode in baseball history has been more discussed, more rehashed, and more debated than the throwing of the
1919 World Series by members of the A.L. champion Chicago White Sox. Even prior to 1919, allegations of the fixing of
baseball games had been swirling around baseball for years, and the White Sox—owned by the notoriously penurious
Charles Comiskey—were a ripe target for gamblers looking for guaranteed winnings. What is often forgotten, however, is
the venom with which the baseball establishment and its friends in the press fought against any investigation of the
rumored scandal, helping prevent details of the fix from emerging for almost a year after the Series. And the scandal's
ramifications—particularly the appointment of Judge Kenesaw Mountain Landis, baseball's first all-powerful
commissioner, to restore the game's integrity—are still being felt today.

"Crookedness and Baseball Do Not Mix"

Just months before the White Sox threw the World Series, *"Commy"* (1919), a fawning biography of Chicago owner Charles Comiskey written by G. W. Axelson, was published. The following excerpt, from an autobiographical chapter by Comiskey himself, reveals both the man's blinkered view of the game and his resentment of even the low wages he paid his players.

White Sox owner Charles Comiskey.

To me baseball is as honorable as any other business. It is the most honest pastime in the world. It has to be or it could not last a season out. Crookedness and baseball do not mix. It has become immeasurably more popular as the years have gone by. It will be greater yet. This year, 1919, is the greatest season of them all.

The reason for the popularity of the sport is that it fits in with the temperament of the American people and because it is on the square. Everything is done in the open. What the magnates do behind the screens the fans care nothing about.

Year by year a higher and higher class of players come into the game. This is not meant as a slur on those of the earlier days, the pioneers, but it is a proof of the attraction it has for young men. The rewards of today are, of course, more in keeping with the efforts than was the case when I broke into the game. I started in at $3 a day. Now some players get that much in a minute, counting their actual playing time.

The Whistle Blower

Hugh S. Fullerton was the first journalist to blow the whistle on the crooked Series, almost a year before details of the scandal became known. The following passages appeared in the *New York Evening World* (December 15, 1919).

Journalist Hugh Fullerton, who exposed the scandal.

Opposite: The 1919 White Sox (above) and Hal Chase, always close by when trouble was brewing.

Professional baseball has reached a crisis. The major leagues, both owners and players, are on trial. Charges of crookedness among the owners, accusations of cheating, of tampering with each other's teams, with attempting to syndicate and control baseball, are bandied about openly. Charges that gamblers have succeeded in bribing ballplayers, that games have been bought and sold, that players are in the pay of professional gamblers and that even the World's Series was tampered with are made without attempt at refutation by the men who have their fortunes invested in baseball. . . .

In the last World's Series the charge was made that seven members of the Chicago White Sox team entered into a conspiracy with certain gamblers to throw the series. I have steadfastly refused to believe this possible. Some of the men whose names are used are my friends and men I would trust anywhere, yet the story is told openly, with so much circumstantial evidence and with so many names, places and dates, that one is bewildered. . . .

Twenty minutes before the final game in Chicago started I was taken aside by a gambler, who told me to plunge. I was mad by that time, and demanded that he come through with some proof or shut his mouth, that he was a crook and accusing others. He laughed and remarked:

"You ought to have cleaned up on it—tipping one team and playing the other."

I was mad all the way through, but wanted to learn something so asked:

"What do you know about today?"

"It'll be the biggest first inning you ever saw," he said.

"Who Is Hugh Fullerton Anyway?"

The Sporting News, Baseball Magazine, and many newspapers excoriated Fullerton for what they labeled his irresponsible (even libelous) charges. The following, a typical response, appeared on the editorial page of *Baseball Magazine* (February 1920).

Who is Hugh Fullerton anyway? A visionary and erratic writer noted for two things: First, his celebrated system for doping plays and players whereby he modestly attempts to foretell (erroneously) not only which team will win a series but exactly how many runs and hits will be made game by game. Second for his proclivity in writing sensational stories usually with the vaguest foundation. . . .

It is possible, as he asserts, that there may be a few players in baseball crooked enough to throw a game, if they could and dared. There will always be a few crooks in every sport. The inherent difficulty of throwing a game, however, is so great, as has been repeatedly shown in this magazine, that it makes the risk practically negligible. Mr. Fullerton knows this as well as anyone and for that reason his wholesale vicious charges are all the more inexcusable.

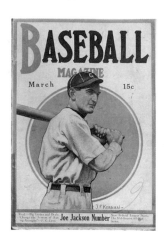

Joe Jackson in happier days
(above and right, flanked by Hall
of Famers Ty Cobb and Wahoo
Sam Crawford).

The Stars Confess

Eventually the truth came out, with White Sox star Eddie Cicotte and others providing the details. From the 1921
Reach Guide.

> Pitcher Cicotte, with tears in his eyes, made the first confession. He told the grand jury
> that he received $10,000 for his part in losing the series, and the money was placed
> under his pillow in his hotel room the night before the first World's Series game in
> Cincinnati. He said he lobbed the ball to the plate so slowly "you could read the trade-
> mark on it" in the first game at Cincinnati, when he was taken out of the box after
> three and two-thirds innings had been played. . . . Outfielder Jackson testified that he
> got $5,000 for throwing the games. . . . Jackson also said that throughout the series he
> either struck out or else hit easy balls when hits would have meant runs.

Judge Landis's Decree

But the players recanted their confessions, crucial evidence disappeared, and all the accused players were acquitted in
court. The 1922 *Reach Guide,* however, showed that the old ways, when ownership winked at corrupt players, were
gone forever—as new commissioner Kenesaw Mountain Landis refused to let the court's acquittal prevent him from
banishing the Chicago players.

> After a charge by Judge Friend the jury retired, and after one ballot, reached a verdict
> of acquittal of all the defendants. . . . When the defendants crowded up to the jury box,
> each man thanked the jury men, and a general jubilation followed, in which the Court

bailiffs joined without being checked by Judge Friend. Subsequently the jury and the acquitted ball players met at a little Italian restaurant on the West Side and there ensued a jollification which lasted most of the night. At this meeting each of the freed ball players expressed the belief that sooner or later he would be back in organized ball, third baseman Weaver being especially confident on this point.

If the players really had any illusions on the subject of a return to organized ball they were quickly dispelled by Commissioner Landis, who said: "Regardless of the verdict of juries, no player that throws a ball game, no player that entertains proposals or promises to throw a game, no player that sits in a conference with a bunch of crooked players and gamblers where the ways and means of throwing games are discussed, and does not promptly tell his club about it, will ever play professional base ball."

Buck Weaver Asks Why

All the banned players felt that they had gotten a raw deal. None, though, was more resentful than Buck Weaver, who did not participate in the fix, though he had knowledge of it. This pointed—if creatively spelled— letter, written to Commissioner Ford Frick thirty-four years after the scandal, shows that Weaver's anger and confusion still burned as if the perceived injustice had happened the day before.

Buck Weaver in 1919.

Dear Sir

I signed a contract in 1919 for three years. I played Ball for Comisky 1919 and 1920 untill the last three games of 1920. Then I was suspended for doing some thing wrong which I new nothing about. I played the 1919 World Series and played a perfect Series.

I also hit around 340.

I stood trial and was acquitted.

You know Commission the only thing we have left in this world is our judge and the 12 jurors and they found me not guilty.

They do some funny things in Base Ball.

Mr. Commission I filed suit for my 1921 contract. Mr. Frick if I was guilty I should never get a penny for my 1921 contract. But Commission they settled for my 1921 contract that makes me right and Comiskey wrong.

So Commission I am asking for reinstatement into organized Base Ball.

Yours Very Truly

George Buck Weaver

PART THREE

1921–1945:
THE GAME IN
ITS GLORY

As the 1920 season came to an end, major league baseball was reeling. The Black Sox scandal, bubbling under the game's surface for almost a year, was finally out in the open—and none of the game's officials escaped the scandal's taint. Suspicions rose that White Sox owner Charles Comiskey and others hadn't investigated the rumors quickly or seriously enough, although *The Sporting News, Baseball Magazine,* and other publications defended the officials' actions. (Albeit with amusingly faint praise: "Magnates honest, even if some are weak or narrow," read one *Sporting News* headline.)

Even Ban Johnson seemed uncharacteristically chastened. "It is quite possible that my conduct in this case was not so energetic as the situation demanded," the American League president admitted.

Judge Kenesaw Mountain Landis.

In the unsavory climate that suddenly afflicted baseball, it became clear to all that the game needed a new guardian, a man of unimpeachable honesty. The choice, after painfully extended debate: Kenesaw Mountain Landis, the controversial federal judge known for his stern visage, unwavering opinions, and moral probity.

Landis, baseball's first and only true czar, ruled with absolute authority for more than two decades. He decreed that baseball players must follow a code of conduct far stricter than that dictated by mere law, ignoring the acquittal in court of the Black Sox players and making sure they remained suspended for life. During his tenure, he frequently acted as judge, jury, and dispenser of justice, suspending, fining, and even banning players for offenses ranging from gambling to postseason barnstorming.

Even the game's superstars were not immune to Landis's iron hand. When Babe Ruth defied the rules and went on a barnstorming trip after the 1921 season, Landis was incensed. "Who does that big monkey think he is?" the judge said, as quoted in J. G. Taylor Spink's *Judge Landis and Twenty-Five Years of Baseball* (1947). "It seems I'll have to show somebody who is running this game." And he did, suspending Ruth and two other transgressors until May 20 of the following season.

Burleigh Grimes, who was allowed to continue to throw a "disgustingly unhygienic" pitch.

Landis's shock therapy for baseball did not eliminate corruption among players or officials, of course. But there is no doubt that his strong will and grand gestures helped restore fans' faith in a game that sorely needed to prove that faith was warranted.

While the new commissioner was beginning to set baseball's front office in order, other forces were conspiring to transform the game on the field. Perhaps most important was a host of rules changes, first instituted in the late 1910s and expanded and enforced after the 1920 season. These changes were a direct result of the beaning death of Ray Chapman and helped bring to an end the pitching- and speed-dominated "dead ball" era.

Most of these rules changes sought to outlaw the spitball and such "freak" deliveries as the shine and emery ball, all of which required the pitcher to tamper with the ball in some way, and all of which were considered difficult to control and a potential danger to the batter. Freak pitches were also considered un-American in their trickiness, and the spitball in particular was said to be "disgustingly unhygienic."

Carl Mays himself apparently did not throw any of these trick pitches; his submarine delivery made the ball difficult to spot, and it appeared to witnesses that Chapman merely froze as the ball approached. No matter: Chapman's death led to cries to enforce a ban on all "underhanded" deliveries.

Howls rose from the pitchers who had openly been relying on the spitter for years. "If they abolish the spit ball they will turn pitching in both leagues bottom side up," moaned Cleveland star Stanley Coveleski. "It is all just as well for fellows like Walter Johnson to say they never use the spit ball and don't need to, but how many pitchers have Johnson's speed?"

In the end, Coveleski, Burleigh Grimes, and a few other established spitballers were allowed to continue to throw the pitch, but no one else was. Within a few years, a batter could dig in at the plate without worrying about a wild, wet one hurtling toward his head.

Another rule change may have been even more important. Chapman had been killed by a stained, dirty ball, which until his death was typical of balls allowed to remain in play. (Baseballs, in fact, were deliberately discolored by the team in the field to aid their pitcher.) But now clean, white balls—far easier for the batter to see—were brought into the game much more frequently.

No one took greater advantage of the new, more visible ball than Babe Ruth. In 1920, before many of these rules were in effect, he had crashed an amazing fifty-four home runs, shattering his league record of twenty-nine. As Bill James points out, if not for the disorienting effects of the Black Sox scandal and Ray Chapman's death, the owners might well have taken "some action to control this obscene burst of offensive productivity, and keep Ruth from making a mockery of the game."

Instead, they instituted the new rules, all of which in effect reduced the pitcher's arsenal and improved the hitter's chances of making solid contact. As *Baseball Magazine*'s editors put it: "'Down with the spitter and on with the base hit,' for a faster, livelier, and more spectacular game."

That's certainly what they got. The extent to which offense dominated the 1920s and 1930s (now known as the lively ball era) is, even today, hard to comprehend. Babe Ruth may have led the league in home runs most years, but he was far from the

STRENGTH

Vol. VI. No. 2   OCTOBER, 1921   Price, 15 Cents

What's Wrong
With the
Skinny Man?

Athletics for
Health and
Efficiency
By WALTER CAMP

Is Boxing
a Health
Destroyer?

Seventy-Seven—
and Still
Going Strong

BABE RUTH

The Magazine of Good Health

*Babe Ruth—easily the most prominent
star of the lively ball era.*

only slugger feasting on the overmatched hurlers' offerings. What follows are just a few of the era's remarkable statistics.

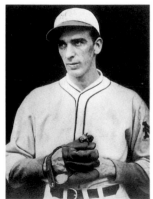

The Giants' Carl Hubbell, who won 253 games and a place in the Hall of Fame—despite pitching against many of the game's most powerful sluggers.

• From 1921 to 1930, neither *league* batted under .280. In 1930, the entire National League—from sluggers to scrubs—batted .303.

• When Ty Cobb batted .401 in 1922, he finished second in the American League, nowhere near league leader George Sisler, who hit .420. Freddie Lindstrom's .379 in 1930 was only good enough for fifth place in the National League race.

• Lou Gehrig drove in 174 runs in 1930 and finished sixteen RBI behind league leader Hack Wilson. Overall, the top eleven single-season RBI totals of all time, ranging from Wilson's 190 in 1930 to Joe DiMaggio's 167 in 1937, occurred during this era.

On the other hand:

• In the American League in 1918, every team posted an ERA of 3.40 or less, and five of the eight teams had ERAs under 3.00. Three years later, the best ERA in the league was 3.79, and four teams couldn't get below 4.00.

• Hall of Famer Carl Hubbell finished second in the National League with a 3.76 ERA in 1930. Brooklyn led the league in team ERA that year at 4.03, while the Giants, who won the N.L. pennant that year, posted a 4.59 mark.

George Sisler, just one of the sluggers who gave pitchers nightmares.

Opposite: Hall of Famer Lefty Gomez, also known as Goofy.

The pitchers of the 1920s and '30s must often have woken in the dark of night, thinking they'd been having bad dreams, and then realized with a shudder that real life was a pitcher's worst nightmare. But batters loved the offense-happy new game—and, more importantly, so did the fans. Attendance grew throughout the 1920s, and it might have kept on growing if not for the beginning of the Great Depression at the end of the decade.

What the fans saw were many of the most colorful and distinctive players in the history of the game. Babe Ruth was the era's great personality, of course, but there were many others who remain nearly as vivid in our memories. St. Louis fans in the thirties knew that they'd have never a dull moment from the talkative and erratic Dizzy Dean, while Dazzy Vance, Gabby Hartnett, and Lefty Gomez also parlayed great skills and famously ebullient personalities into Hall of Fame membership.

Of course, not all of the era's superstars presented such a cheerful demeanor. Rogers Hornsby, for example, averaged .382 during the 1920s while making enemies wherever he played, and Lefty Grove won 300 games, while being (as *The Ultimate Baseball Book* put it) "so unfathomably angry in defeat that his teammates couldn't go near him."

Others let their on-field accomplishments speak for them. Lou Gehrig provided the reserved counterpoint to the Babe's bluster, and other quiet warriors included Mel Ott, Jimmie Foxx, Charlie Gehringer, Tony Lazzeri, and many others whose images have faded a bit from our minds as the years have passed.

Baseball, like all industries, struggled during the depression. As the 1930s drew to a close, though, attendance seemed to be recovering—but at that moment forces far larger than the game were heralding the end of a remarkably calm time in the game's history.

The first shock was Lou Gehrig's sudden retirement in 1939, followed by his death on June 2, 1941. Gehrig was not the first player, or even the first star, to die young and tragically, but his death seemed to hurt worse than the others. If the Iron Horse could be struck down, logic said, any one of us could too.

Gehrig's illness and death coincided with the onset and expansion of World War II in Europe. Although the U.S. hadn't yet become directly involved, it was impossible not to realize that no matter how much we wanted to pretend that our lives—and our pastimes—were untouched by the war, thousands of men and women were dying in the fight against a dictator just across the Atlantic.

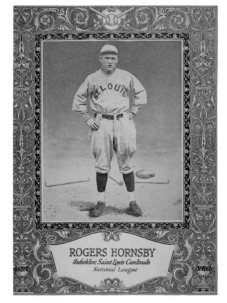

The aggressive and brilliant Rogers Hornsby.

Then, on December 7, 1941, the Japanese bombed Pearl Harbor. Two days later, columnist Shirley Povich wrote in *The Washington Post,* "[I]f the baseball people don't recognize this week's outbreak as a powerful threat to their game we've been wrong all these years in calling them pretty smart folks."

Baseball people *did* realize it, and even debated shutting the game down for the duration—until President Roosevelt sent his famous letter to Commissioner Landis on January 15, 1942, commanding that the game continue. Roosevelt's quid pro quo for this green light was that "players who are of active military or naval age should go, without question, into the service." And go they did: Hank Greenberg, Ted Williams, Stan Musial, Bob Feller, Johnny Mize, and dozens of lesser players enlisted. Many, including Greenberg and Williams, spent the duration of the war in the service, sacrificing as many as four seasons of their careers for their country.

The major league teams were forced to scramble to replace departed players on their rosters. Today, the war years in baseball are looked back upon as a slightly embarrassing interlude in the course of the great game. It's true that the teams were increasingly forced to sign washed-up old ballplayers and unseasoned kids, and it's also true that the 1945 St. Louis Browns played Pete Gray, a one-armed outfielder (who hit only .218, but did have three outfield assists).

But it's not true that wartime baseball was a farce. To make up for the players' limitations, reflected in declining batting averages and power numbers (for example, the American League as a whole hit 883 home runs in 1940, but

only 430 in 1945), the wartime game substituted a great deal of baserunning and other strategy. Some good pennant races and even the arrival of such future stars as Allie Reynolds and Eddie Stanky meant that baseball between 1942 and 1945 wasn't nearly as woeful as it's remembered to be.

Two moments in Lou Gehrig's all-too-short life. "Gehrig's hands are like an iron vise and his arms are as big as many a man's leg," wrote F. C. Lane of the slugger in his prime (opposite). Above: Gehrig on July 4, 1939, the day he retired.

Top: Yankee Stadium was where you found it—even North Africa—during the war.

When the war ended, and the stars and other players came home, however, most of the players who had filled in disappeared quickly from the majors. The game was once again populated by the great players of prewar days—as well as a growing number of young stars. And the public, filled with the new hope and new prosperity that peace had brought, was ready.

Baseball's next great leap forward in popularity was about to begin.

"JUDGE LANDIS: BASEBALL'S STERN SAVIOR"

Kenesaw Mountain Landis, named commissioner of baseball in the wake of the 1919 Black Sox scandal, presided for more than twenty years. During this time he made plenty of enemies—including, at one time or another, many of the owners and several star ballplayers, including Babe Ruth. But as Frank Graham's eulogy, originally printed in *Baseball Magazine* (February 1945), shows, the game's custodians never forgot what they owed Landis.

A shock of gray hair, a piercing eye, a scowl and a rasping voice, a rumpled hat and a stick and rumpled top coat with the collar turned up—these were the props that Kenesaw Mountain Landis used to fashion himself into a character. He was as much of an actor as the late Frank Bacon, whom he loved—or George Raft, whom he detested. He knew how to catch the limelight and the headlines and his gestures and expressions were such that sometimes you were tempted to believe he rehearsed them. But behind his make-up, the man had a fine, alert mind and a special talent for the job he took over in 1920 and managed skilfully to the day of his death. He was a great man for baseball and the debt it owes him is so tremendous it never can be paid.

The game was reeling under the blast fired by the gamblers and their dupes among the ballplayers when he was called in to hold it steady and, by his presence, to re-create public confidence in its honesty. No one else was as well qualified for this task as he was. He knew baseball, though no better than millions of other Americans. But, far more important than that, he knew how to deal with the men who made up the professional game—the ballplayers, the managers, the club owners and the league officials. He knew that, with very few exceptions, they were staunchly honest and he knew, too, that they could be very stupid. One thing more he knew: The club owners were in great fear of losing their investments and, in their fear, would be docile in his hands. He applied that knowledge to make himself the absolute master of those who had thought only to use him for their own benefit—and discovered, too late, that they had sworn just about everything but their lives into his keeping.

Major league owners gave Judge Landis (seated, center) almost absolute power.

The Judge clearly established the position of the club owners the day they approached him, literally with their hats in their hands, to offer him the post as commissioner. They were in session in Chicago and, at the suggestion of Al Lasker, a large stock holder in the Chicago National League club, had agreed that he was the man they sorely needed. When they got in touch with him and wanted to know if he would discuss the matter with them, he told them he would, adding shrewdly that, if they liked, they might call on him immediately in his court room in the Federal Building.

It never occurred to them that they were playing into his hands when they accepted the invitation. But he put them in their places the moment they walked into the court room. He was hearing a case and paid not the slightest heed to them as they entered, affecting not to know who they were or even that they were there. He must have laughed inwardly at the sight of them, huddled in the back of the room, clutching their hats. And when they shuffled their feet nervously, he looked at them and said, harshly:

"Unless that noise ceases, I shall have to clear the court room."

They were licked right there and they must have known it, because when he finally condescended to talk to them and said he would take the job, they virtually signed their rights and properties over to him, lock, stock and barrel. And in the years to come, when they were restless in the grip he had fastened upon them, he had only to call them together and read the riot act to them to quiet them. Once or twice he threatened to resign and that made them panicky, for it was a dreadful threat. They knew that if he actually resigned, his action would condemn them in the public mind. He had them there.

This was a hard state of affairs, seemingly unreasonable, definitely un-American and all that sort of thing. And yet it was the only way in which he could manage a job no one ever had attempted before and for which there were no rules or regulations. There was much that he had to do right from the beginning, and he plunged enthusiastically and sometimes stubbornly into the task, making up his rules as he went along. He did not lack for active opposition. . . .

But, through all his career as commissioner, he had two great forces on his side: the ballplayers and the public. The ballplayers knew that he genuinely was their friend and could be depended upon to uphold their rights in conflict with their employers. The public looked upon him as a savior of the game, which he was. In the main, he had the support of the sports writers, too. They quarreled with him now and then, hit at some of his decisions, and pointed out his mistakes, but with very few exceptions they had implicit confidence in him and a great personal liking for him.

As the years went on, he mellowed but never weakened. He worked hard at his job, enjoyed it, got some amusement out of it, could be hard and tough about it. Perhaps not all his judgments were sound but he was like an umpire who calls the plays as he sees them and, believing he is right, defends himself vigorously against his critics. One decision saddened him greatly. This was his banishment of Jimmy O'Connell of the Giants, who admitted that before a game in the closing week of the 1924 season, he had offered Heinie Sand, the Phillies' shortstop, $500 not to "bear down" against the Giants. Jimmy was an extremely likable and naive young man and it was suspected that he was the victim of a plot—or a hoax, equally cruel. Friends of the Judge's pleaded with him, a year or so later, to allow O'Connell to return to baseball.

"No," he said. "I can't. I have given this matter more thought than you or any one

else and I, too, am deeply sorry for O'Connell. I would give anything on earth if I could see a way to reinstate him but I simply can't. Baseball is bigger than O'Connell—and bigger than I. It was a sorry decision I had to make but I must stand by it."

In recent years he developed a phobia on the subject of race track betting, seeking to prevent ballplayers and umpires from attending the races, chasing Rogers Hornsby out of the major leagues and preventing even such reputable figures as Alfred Gwynne Vanderbilt and Bing Crosby from buying into major league clubs. Yet he felt that this was justified because he believed there was a link between race track gambling and that measure of dishonesty in baseball that he had been called upon to stamp out. He was no enemy of the tracks in the days when he was a Federal judge but used to go to the races and, to the very end of his life, counted as one of his best friends Col. Matt Winn of Kentucky Derby fame. He simply recognized a danger and fought sternly to repress it. . . .

Now that he is gone, there can be no replacement for him. For one thing, there is no longer need for a policeman at the top of baseball—and call him what you would, that's what he was. For another, there is no one else like him. Eventually the club owners will get around to appointing another commissioner but he will not have the power that Landis wielded nor will he—no matter who he is—even remotely resemble Landis.

The Judge was a fabulous figure whose life followed a fabulous course. A brilliant but erratic jurist whose decisions frequently were overruled by the higher courts—even the famous $29,000,000 fine he slapped on the Standard Oil Company failed to stick—he probably would have remained on the Federal bench to the end of his days if the White Sox hadn't tossed the 1919 series. There was no way in which he possibly could have prepared himself consciously for the job as baseball commissioner and yet when it came to him he was ready for it. Whether or not he ever thought of himself as such, he was a man of destiny.

THE ONE, THE ONLY

No player in the history of the game garnered more publicity—or deserved it more—than Babe Ruth. The Babe spent much of his childhood—and learned to love baseball—in St. Mary's Industrial School in Baltimore, where he had been sent by his parents for uncontrollable behavior. Though others may have seen the boarding school as a prison, as Robert Creamer says in *Babe* (1974), Ruth "looked back on St. Mary's later with a warmth and nostalgia he never felt for the places he lived with his family. St. Mary's was his home."

Life at St. Mary's
From George Herman Ruth, *Babe Ruth's Own Book of Baseball* (1928)

My earliest recollections center about the dirty, traffic-crowded streets of Baltimore's river front.

Crowded streets they were too, noisy with the roar of heavy trucks whose drivers cursed and swore and aimed blows with their driving whips, at the legs of kids who made the streets their playground.

And the youngsters, running wild, struck back and echoed the curses. Truck-drivers were our enemies: so were the coppers patrolling their beats and so too were the shopkeepers who took bruising payment from our skins for the apples and the fruit we "snitched" from their stands and counters.

Opposite: Judge Landis (center) enjoying a game the old-fashioned way—through a knothole.

A rough, tough neighborhood, but I liked it.

There in those crooked winding streets I staged my first fight, and lost it, I think. There too I played my first baseball. There I learned to fear and to hate the coppers. Perhaps it was there, too, that I learned to control my pitches. For tossing overripe apples, or aged eggs at a truck driver's head is mighty good practice—although I don't recommend it to the boys of today.

Many people thought I was an orphan. I wasn't. My folks lived in Baltimore and my father worked in the district where I was raised. We were poor. Very poor. And there were times when we never knew where the next meal was coming from. But I never minded. I was no worse off than the other kids with whom I played and fought.

I don't know how I happened to be sent to St. Mary's school. As a matter of fact it wasn't so much a school as it was a home where kids like me could be cared for and trained and taught as they should be. All I remember is that I was a loose jointed, gangling dirty-faced kid in knee pants playing in the street, where one day a round-faced pleasant little man in clerical garb came over to talk to me.

I thought he was a priest and I called him Father, and tipped my cap when I spoke to him.

"Not Father," he said, smiling, "Just Brother—Brother Gilbert."

Then he told me that I was to go with him, that I would be given a fine home and taught things that would make me into a useful citizen. I didn't want to go. I liked the freedom of the street; liked the gang of youngsters I played with and prowled with.

But I went.

For a while I wasn't happy. I missed the crowds, and the dirt, and the noise of the street. I missed the other kids. I even missed the policemen and the beatings that came

The slim, young Babe Ruth (far right), with other members of the Red Sox's imposing pitching staff.

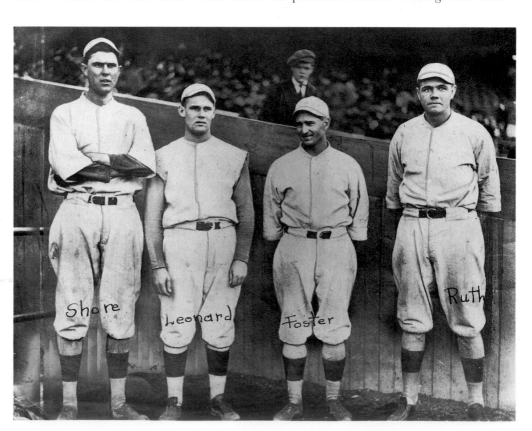

from the shopkeepers when we were unfortunate enough to fall into their clutches. As I look back at it now I realize that I must have been a real problem to the Brothers.

But Brother Gilbert stuck with me. I owe him a lot. More than I'll ever be able to repay.

It was Brother Gilbert who finally struck upon the thing to hold my interest and keep me happy. It was baseball. Once I had been introduced to school athletics I was satisfied and happy. Even as a kid I was big for my years, and because of my size I used to get most any job I liked on the team. Sometimes I pitched. Sometimes I caught, and frequently I played the outfield and infield. It was all the same to me. All I wanted was to play. I didn't care much where.

He Knew His Limitations

Babe Ruth sees the future (written by Ruth in a St. Mary's hymnal):

"George H. Ruth, world's worse singer, world's best pitcher"

The Babe's Debut

Following a short stint with the International League's Baltimore Orioles, the Babe (then, of course, a pitcher) was sold to the Boston Red Sox. Here, a report by Tim Murnane of the *Boston Globe* on Mr. Ruth's first big-league appearance, July 11, 1914.

The Red Sox introduced Mr. Ruth, one of the Baltimore recruits, yesterday to the crowd at Fenway Park and with the assistance of Leonard, the Fresno fruit grower, the young man led the home club over the wire by a score of 4 to 3. There was a fine crowd and they enjoyed the short, snappy contest immensely, as only one hour and 33 minutes were taken up in playing the game.

All eyes were turned on Ruth, the giant left hander, who proved a natural ball player and went through his act like a veteran of many wars. He has a natural delivery, fine control and a curve ball that bothers the batsmen, but has room for improvement and will, undoubtedly, become a fine pitcher under the care of Manager Carrigan.

He held the Naps to five hits in six innings, with one strikeout, but was hit hard in the seventh, when the visitors tied the score by scoring two earned runs on singles by Kirke and Chapman, a sacrifice, and a single by O'Neill. That was the curtain for the Oriole importation, and he looked weak only in comparison with Dutch Leonard, who pitched the last two innings, putting six men out in order, four of them on strikes.

Why I Sold Ruth

When Red Sox owner Harry Frazee sold Babe Ruth to the New York Yankees after the 1919 season, the baseball world was stunned. Ruth, already an acknowledged star, had won nine games that season for the Sox, with an ERA of 2.97. Incidentally, he'd also begun playing the outfield and had slugged twenty-nine home runs (by far the most ever hit in the major leagues at the time), driven in 114 runs, and compiled a .657 slugging average. In the April 1920 *Baseball Magazine,* Frazee recited a familiar set of reasons for his decision to unload the Babe.

Red Sox owner Harry Frazee (second from left), the man who sold Babe Ruth to the New York Yankees, bringing the Curse of the Bambino down on Sox fans.

In explanation, I mention these facts:

1. To my mind, no individual player in so uncertain a profession as baseball is worth any such sum of money [Ruth had asked for $20,000 a year]. Ruth made twenty-nine home runs last year, but no one knows what he will do next year, even if he has good health, and no one can guarantee that he will enjoy good health.

2. Frankly, I felt that I could not afford to pay the huge salary Ruth demanded. New York may be able to do so but I could not. And the complications which would arise with other and more faithful members of the Red Sox would be endless and disastrous.

3. The value of an individual player, however great, may well be exaggerated. If one member of a club dominates public interest to the exclusion of the other members of that club, he may well do more injury than good. Last year, Ruth played wonderful individual ball. But where did the club finish in spite of all his good work? Where would the club have finished had Ruth not been a member of the club? Does anyone think we would not have beaten out the Athletics? Or Washington? I am sure of it and I would have taken my chances on catching up with the St. Louis Browns.

Ruth is a great individual star, one of the greatest in baseball. But the records of the game are full of stars who never get the team anywhere. My sole object, since coming to Boston, has been to give the public a winning team. With the exception of the Ruth deal, everyone will admit that my work has tended to bring about that result. And, personally, I think this latest deal will take its place along with the rest for I believe the sale of Ruth will ultimately strengthen the team.

"And the Game Goes On"

Ruth had his greatest season yet in 1921, hitting fifty-nine home runs and driving in 171 runs for the Yankees. But after the season, in direct defiance of Judge Landis, he chose to embark on a postseason barnstorming trip—and got himself suspended for the first six weeks of the next season for his insubordination. From the 1922 *Reach Guide,* an acerbic, unsigned comment on the imbroglio.

> If Ruth, next May,
> Returns to play
> And knocks 'em far and high,
> The birds will sing
> Their songs of spring
> Beneath a smiling sky.
> If Ruth, next May,
> Declines to play
> As in the days of yore,
> The birds will sing
> Their songs of spring
> As they have sung before.

Pitching to the Babe

By 1923 Ruth was the most feared slugger in baseball history. In November, after a season in which he batted an astounding .393 with forty-one home runs, *Baseball Magazine* published this interview with the brilliant pitcher Urban Shocker, who was coming off his fourth consecutive twenty-win season with the St. Louis Browns. Shocker spoke for every pitcher in the American League.

Urban Shocker, who battled Ruth for years as a pitcher with the St. Louis Browns—and then became his teammate in 1925.

Overleaf: Babe Ruth's mighty swing.

A Major League pitcher has a pretty hard life, all fairy stories to the contrary notwithstanding. He may work only once in three or four days, but he makes up in worry for the days he doesn't work. For he is always tormented by thinking of what might have been if he had pitched that ball that somebody hit for a three-bagger just a little more outside and a shade higher. Besides even if he doesn't hear the criticisms that are made behind his back, and some of them are not always behind his back, a pitcher reads the newspapers and they have a plain way sometimes, those newspaper boys, of telling him just how rotten he is.

Still with all the hard knocks there is some recompense for the down-trodden pitcher. Take Babe Ruth for example. I like to pitch to Babe better than to anybody else in baseball. And I consider him the most dangerous of all batters.

Why do I like to pitch to Babe? Because he is a never-ending puzzle. You always have to extend yourself to the utmost when you face Babe. Sometimes he looks very easy, but there is one thing it is never safe for a pitcher to bank on. Any time he figures that he has Babe's number he is feeding himself a liberal dose of misplaced confidence.

There is one thing that Babe can always be counted upon to supply. He gives the opposing pitcher a thrill no matter what happens. If you strike him out you get a very pleasurable thrill, as long as it lasts. If he hits you for a solid smash you get another kind of a thrill. Why do cowboys ride wild steers and risk their necks on bucking

broncos? It's a dangerous sport but it gives them a thrill, I suppose, to think they have conquered something which was strong and reckless and hard to handle.

Kids, Sisters, and Mothers

From *The New York Yankees: An Informal History* (1943), by Frank Graham, here is another view of the legend.

Ruth was very proud of his baserunning—although it was never the strongest part of his game.

The Babe was—and remains—utterly indifferent to names. To him, any male, regardless of age, is "Kid." A young woman is "Sister," an elderly woman "Mother." Incredible as it may seem, there were times when he didn't know the names of some of his team mates. One day, when Paul Whiteman visited the Yankees in their dugout at the Stadium, the Babe took him down the line of players, introducing him.

"This is Herb Pennock," he said. "And this is Bob Meusel. This is Lou Gehrig and this is—er . . . er . . ."

"Wera," the player said.

"Oh, sure! Wera . . . and this is Earle Combs and this is—er . . .

"Braxton."

"Of course! Braxton. And this is . . ."

Wera and Braxton and a few others. Their proper names simply never had registered with him. He had his own names for them, however. Wera was Flop Ears and Braxton was Chicken Neck. And, incidentally, Shocker was always Rubber Belly.

The Babe with a group of "sisters."

Word was received in Baltimore one early spring day that the Babe would pass through on his way to the South about noon. Paul Minton, a newspaperman, asked Alphonse Thomas, now the manager of the Orioles but then a pitcher with the White Sox but residing in Baltimore, if he wouldn't like to go down the train to say hello to him.

"Sure," Thomas said. "And I'll lay you a little bet he doesn't recognize me or, if he does, he can't call me by name."

Minton thought he was fooling. But he wasn't. When the train stopped and the Babe got off to walk up and down on the station platform for a few minutes, Minton, with Thomas at his side, greeted him.

"How are you, kid!" the Babe said, shaking his hand.

"You remember Alphonse Thomas," Minton said.

"Sure I do," the Babe said, still talking to Minton as the grinning Thomas stood by, completely unnoticed by him. "How are you, Tommy?"

There was the time when, after an extra-inning ball game, he showered and dressed in even greater haste than usual.

"I nearly forgot I had a dinner date," he explained.

"With whom?" Pennock asked.

"That man and woman in the movies," the Babe said.

"What man and woman?"

"Oh, you know. They just got back from Europe."

"Douglas Fairbanks and Mary Pickford, by any chance?"

"That's right," the Babe said, struggling into his coat and rushing for the door. "I never can remember their names."

The chances are that, in the course of the dinner, Doug and Mary were somewhat puzzled at being addressed as Kid and Sister.

September 30, 1927: Ruth slugs number sixty—the most famous home run of all time.

"Ruth Crashes 60th to Set New Record"

The pinnacle of a career, from *The New York Times,* October 1, 1927.

Babe Ruth scaled the hitherto unattained heights yesterday. Home run 60, a terrific smash off the southpaw pitching of Zachary, nestled in the Babe's favorite spot in the right field bleachers, and before the roar had ceased it was found that this drive not only had made home run record history but also was the winning margin in a 4 to 2 victory over the Senators. This also was the Yanks' 109th triumph of the season. Their last league game of the year will be played today.

Babe Ruth being honored at Yankee Stadium two months before his death. "The only real game in the world, I think, is baseball," the Babe once said.

When the Babe stepped to the plate in that momentous eighth inning the score was deadlocked. Koenig was on third base, the result of a triple, one man was out and all was tense. It was the Babe's fourth trip to the plate during the afternoon, a base on balls and two singles resulting on his other visits plateward.

The first Zachary offering was a fast one, which sailed over for a called strike. The next was high. The Babe took a vicious swing at the third pitched ball and the bat connected with a crash that was audible in all parts of the stand. It was not necessary to follow the course of the ball. The boys in the bleachers indicated the route of the record homer. It dropped about half way to the top. No. 60 was some homer, a fitting wallop to top the Babe's record of 59 in 1921.

While the crowd cheered and the Yankee players roared their greetings the Babe made his triumphant, almost regal tour of the paths. He jogged around slowly, touched each bag firmly and carefully and when he imbedded his spikes in the rubber disk to record officially Homer 60, hats were tossed into the air, papers were torn up and tossed liberally and the spirit of celebration permeated the place.

The Babe's stroll out to his position was the signal for a handkerchief salute in which all the bleacherites, to the last man, participated. Jovial Babe entered into the carnival spirit and punctuated his Kingly strides with a succession of snappy military salutes.

1923: THE YANKEE DYNASTY BEGINS

A report on the first of twenty World Series victories in the next forty seasons, from the elegant pen of Grantland Rice, originally published in his *Sportlights of 1923* (1924).

The Yankees rode through the storm at last to reach the shining haven where the gold dust for the winter's end lies ankle-deep in the streets.

Trailing by three runs at the end of the seventh inning of the world's series game, with Art Nehf in supreme command of their waning destinies, they came through shadows as black as the heart of Stygia to find for the first time the radiant sunlight of a championship.

Babe Ruth beating the throw back to first during the 1923 Series.

In its first year, Yankee Stadium—the House that Ruth Built—welcomed fans to the third straight Yank-Dodger World Series. "Let's hope both New York clubs will be well whipped in 1924," wrote W. A. Phelon in Baseball Magazine, *"and that the flags will fly in two new cities."*

For the third straight afternoon the aroused Yankees beat the Giants, this time by 6 to 4, in a ball game that reeked with drama from a thousand open pores.

There have been great games before in this amazing series, but nothing even to approach the melodramatic upheaval that brought the Yankees to triumph in the eighth frame. For in this eighth inning there were massed and concentrated the fall of Rome, the destruction of Carthage, the feast of Belshazzar, the rout of Cyrus, the march of Attila, the wreck of the Hesperus and the Chicago fire.

Almost every element that tends to churn human emotions into a froth and starts the pulse jumping sideways struck the scene in this wild and woolly inning before the last Yankee was retired. There has been nothing like it in a pastime that has rung in sudden changes upon 10,000 themes. Nothing quite like it through a year of drama that in almost every branch of sport has lifted the human scalp up and down like flapjacks tossed by the camp cook in the heart of the piney woods.

When the rally ended, which carried the Yankees from defeat to victory, there was hardly a thumping heart in the park that wasn't pumped dry of blood as the crowd sank back, limp and exhausted from the nerve-wrecking strain.

The crash came with the startling suddenness of a simoon across the Indian Ocean, where the simoon has its lair. When the Yankees came to bat in the eighth the Giants were leading 4 to 1, with Art Nehf in one of his most brilliant moods. With the exception of a pass to Babe Ruth in the fourth Nehf had retired sixteen Yankees in unbroken order, rolling them back as some great cliff would turn back the summer's surf. They were breaking in vain against his speed, curves and control, while Giant batsmen were nicking Herb Pennock from round to round with an even, steady bombardment led by the spectacular Frisch.

Outside of Babe Ruth's home run in the first, a wallop that broke two records, and Ward's single in the second Nehf had allowed nothing like a hit. But as the finish drew near only his steel-spun nerve was holding him up. His face was beginning to show signs of the crushing strain, as he came in after the seventh white and drawn. But he had held Yankee hitters in such complete subjection to his wiry left wrist that no one

Giant Casey Stengel scores after hitting an inside-the-park home run in the ninth inning of Game One, providing the margin of victory in a 5–4 win.

Opposite: Wally Pipp and Aaron Ward coming around to score on Deacon Scott's single in Game Four. The Yanks' 8–4 victory knotted the Series at two games apiece.

looked for anything approaching the debacle that followed. Ward was the first to face Nehf in the eighth, and he popped out. He was the twelfth Yankee in succession that had been turned back from first.

With Ward out Schang singled, the first Yankee hit since the second inning. But it was not until Deacon Scott followed with another smashing punch to safe terrain that the crowd came to its feet with the call of the wild. There was then the scent of carnage in the air, the indefinable something that tips off the approaching hurricane.

The weary Nehf, now completely fagged, pitched four successive balls to Hofmann, who had supplanted Pennock at bat. By now, with the bases filled and only one out, the crowd was a seething caldron of riot and action, great stuff for a mob scene picture of the French Revolution. Nehf's last stand was one of the tragedies of sport. From the heights of the conqueror he had dropped within three minutes to the rocks below, as if fate had pushed him from the ledge just as he was crossing the final gap. With this control still broken he then passed Joe Bush, batting for Whitey Witt, forcing Schang over the plate, and leaving the bases still full.

Eight successive balls ended Nehf's work for the year. He came from the field with bowed head, wiping the grimy sweat from his eyes with his gloved hand, moving as a man walks to the guillotine or the chair.

You can imagine the scene at this moment, with Rosy Ryan standing in the box as Joe Dugan came to bat. Ryan, picking up where Nehf left off, added another pass without throwing a strike, forcing in another run. Nehf and Ryan together had now missed the plate twelve times in a row—one of the most amazing lapses of control ever seen in any game, from the bush to the big tent. Twelve balls without a strike may not be a record, but it isn't far away.

Still the drama grew in tensity. For here was Babe Ruth at bat, with the bases filled and two runs needed to win—Ruth standing "amid the alien corn," as Keats once put it, yearning "for home."

And it was here that Ryan for a moment almost saved the day. Ruth took two vicious cuts, fouled and missed. The next was a ball. Then Ryan, coming up on his toes, broke over a fast, deep curve ball that also came near breaking Ruth's heart. The home-run maker, lashing with full power, struck empty October air as the ball broke a full foot below his whistling mace for the third strike.

Oh, what a fall was that, my countrymen! No wonder here that Giant rooters arose en masse with the shrill clamor of the tribe, as Yankee rooters, dumbfounded by the sudden turn, caught their throats with shaking hands. For there were now two out, and if Ryan could only retire Bob Meusel the game was safe, after all, with the Giants still a run beyond. Ruth, after the greatest world's series ball he had ever played, was almost as broken and dejected as Nehf as he stalked back to the dugout, knowing that if Meusel failed the king would be a goat within the few tickings of a watch.

But Ryan for the moment had pitched his soul away to strike out Ruth. Meusel, amid the reverberating clamor of the multitude, ripped a sharp bounder through the box.

The ball hopped just beyond the Giant's reach and scampered on to center field as Haines, running for Hofmann, and Johnson, running for Bush, scored with waving arms.

This $50,000 blow broke up the battle with all further doubt removed when Cunningham's throw to third bounded past Groh and Dugan also crossed the plate with the fifth run of the famous round.

1926: JOHN J. KNEW . . . SOMETIMES

After more than thirty years in the game, Giant manager John McGraw considered himself a pretty fair judge of talent. In this March 1926 letter to the Giants' owner, Charles A. Stoneham, he describes two untested young players. One, Mel Ott, would go on to hit 511 career home runs, score 1859 and drive in 1861 runs, and march into the Hall of Fame on the first ballot. The other, a man named Fay Thomas, ended a four-year major league career with a record of 9–20, and an ERA of 4.95.

Mel Ott in 1926.

Dear Mr. Stoneham:

Here is a hurried description of the player question.

Ott and Thomas are stand-outs with me, and in one year should be a great help to this team. Thomas has more stuff than [any] young pitcher I have seen since Mathewson. A little green but I think has plenty of Heart. Ott is the best looking young player at the bat in my time with the Club. I am going to try to make an outfielder out of him.

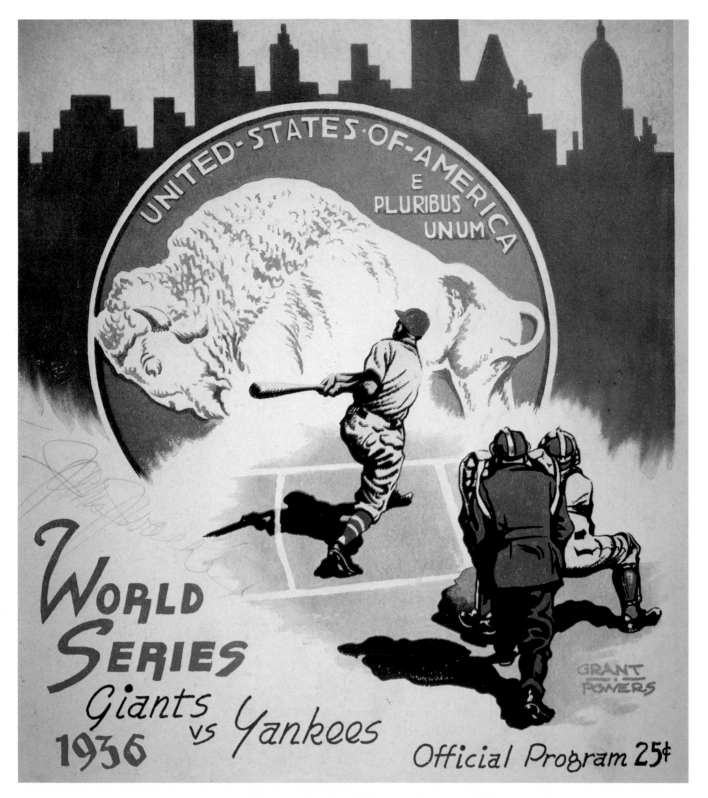

Mel Ott batted .304 in the 1936 Series, but the Giants still fell to the hated Yankees in six games.

"DIZZY" DEAN

IN A
FULL
PAGE
OF

PHOTOGRAVURE

Saturday's DAILY NEWS

1930: DIZZY DEAN EARNS HIS REPUTATION

Even people who never saw him play know that Ol' Diz was one of the game's true characters—witty, outspoken, and always unpredictable. As demonstrated in this charming story by Ken Chilcote, which appeared in *The Sporting News* on October 9, 1930, even as a nineteen-year-old rookie, Dizzy was quite willing to take on St. Louis Cardinals' front-office executive Branch Rickey, manager Gabby Street—and the press.

A ready smile, a stream of palaver, and terrific stuff: The incomparable Dizzy Dean.

St. Joseph, Mo.—He may be the dazzler now, but he'll always be known as Dizzy Dean hereabouts. The six-foot prospect belonging to the Cardinals arrived in town this week and delighted in telling everyone what a snap the big leagues are. After pitching one game for the Cardinals on the last day of the season and winning, 3 to 1, over the Pittsburg Pirates, the chesty Texan now brags, "show me another pitcher in the majors who has never been defeated."

And September 28, when the Cardinals entrained for Philadelphia, at the close of the season, Dizzy took a different train and came to St. Joseph, where he got his start in the Western League this year.

"Sure they begged and begged me to go along with them," he declared soon after his arrival·here. "But you know I'm fed up on this baseball stuff. Us big league pitchers get rather bored in time.

"I told Mr. Rickey I would wait until next year and win him three games in the World's Series. I would have done that this year, if they'd allowed me to work. It sure was a shame that I had to help out the [minor league] Houston club in place of going to the Cards in time to work in the series.

"Nope, I've never seen a World's Series and I don't think there is anything there that would interest me this year. Gee, I'll bet a lot of St. Louis people wish I was pitching every game.

"Down there they think I'm good. Well, after seeing several of the big league teams play while with the Cards the last half of the season, I don't recall seeing any better than myself. I told Gabby I could win him 20 or 30 games next year. And to tell you the truth I don't think I will be beaten.

"Don't think though that I'm bragging about all this, I'm just lettin' you in on some inside facts. Oh yeah, next year I'm going to be known as 'The Great Dean'."

THE SHAPE OF THINGS TO COME: NIGHT BASEBALL

From Clifford Bloodgood, *Baseball Magazine* (April 1931), a glimpse of what would finally reach the majors in 1935.

Late in April, last year, the Independence club and the Muskogee club, of the Western Association, played the first league night baseball game ever staged in America. Within a few weeks minor league owners invited and even implored the manufacturers of flood lights to install their equipment at the various parks. The game, under the electric rays, spread like wildfire through the lesser circuits. From the Atlantic to the Pacific, from Class D leagues to the big Double A circuits, baseball at night took hold. Attendance records swelled and at last the little fellows had something to crow about. They were no longer flirting with the house over the hill.

Naturally this experiment did not pass unnoticed by the major leagues, but it did not win a place of considerable importance in their minds. Many of the major league moguls were frankly skeptical of and some openly hostile to illuminated diamond baseball. They admitted that the night game had exerted a tremendous popular appeal in the minor leagues, especially in the smaller cities, but they were of the opinion that once the novelty wore off the attendance would wane.

Some years ago the home run was a novelty. The fans got such a thrill seeing a base-runner negotiate four sacks on a wallop that they showered him with coins. Today the four-base batting bombardment is so common that not a dime is thrown out for a

Opposite: "The Great Dean" always had time for a chat.

More than twenty thousand fans showed up at Crosley Field in Cincinnati on May 24, 1935, to watch the Reds play the Phillies in the first major league night game.

carload and the hit has lost its novelty appeal. But have the major league fans stayed away because of this thumping? A bumper crop of rooters turned out last year and got torrid about the home run feuds. The merry battle between Hack Wilson and Babe Ruth for the H. R. crown drew almost as much interest as the pennant races in some major league quarters. . . .

Once baseball has been permanently established in the smaller cities under the glaring lights will the major leagues still voice their displeasure? Undoubtedly, but just as surely, in time, they will install artificial lighting systems in their own major league parks.

NICKNAMES IN THE 1930S

Every era was characterized by the type of nicknames players hung on each other. In *The Bill James Historical Baseball Abstract* (1985), James illustrates the malign creativity of a uncetain age.

Nicknames in the thirties got nasty. There have always been a few less-than-complimentary nicknames around, sometimes more than a few, but in the thirties, under the pressure of economic catastrophe on the one hand and journalism as hero-worship on the other, nicknames in large numbers emerged as a way of defining the limitations of one and all. Harry Davis was called "Stinky," Frankie Hayes was called "Blimp," Red Lucas was "The Nashville Narcissus," Ernie Lombardi "Schnozz," and Eric McNair "Boob." Hugh Mulcahy, who lost seventy-six games in four years, was therefore

Above: Fat Freddie Fitzsimmons (right).
Right: Ducky Wucky Medwick.

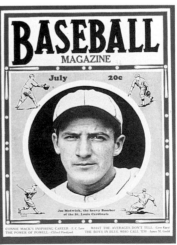

169

Bucketfoot Al Simmons.
Opposite: Dazzy Vance.

called "Losing Pitcher Mulcahy," and Lynn Nelson was called "Line Drive Nelson" because everything he threw up there came rocketing back at him. Walter Beck, a pitcher with a career record of 38–69, was called "Boom Boom."

You didn't want to be fat in this climate, or it became part of your name. Freddie Fitzsimmons, a fine pitcher, was called "Fat Freddie," Babe Phelps was also called "Blimp," Walter Brown was called "Jumbo," and Alfred Dean was "Chubby" Dean. Bob Fothergill, of course, was called "Fatty," and a couple of players were called "Porky." Johnny Riddle was called "Mutt," and Bob Seeds was called "Suitcase" because he was traded or released so often. Nicknames, in this way, tended to call attention not to the player's strengths, but to his weaknesses. Leo Durocher was not "The Little General" or "The Peerless Leader," but "The Lip." Nick Cullop, whose face was beet red, was called "Old Tomato Face." Harvey Hendrick was called "Gink." Sammy Byrd, a defensive replacement for the Bambino, was called "Babe Ruth's Legs," a nickname which has no parallel that I know of (no one was ever called "Mark Belanger's Bat" or anything). Dom Dallessandro was called "Dim Dom," a play on sounds, and Bill Zuber was called "Goober Zuber," a terrific play on sounds but, again, not high on my list of things I should like to be known as.

In this context, even nicknames that were intended to be complimentary, or at least innocent, start to sound suspicious. Morrie Arnovich was "Snooker." Harry Danning was "Harry the Horse." Odell Hale was "Bad News." Dick Bartell was "Rowdy Richard." George Selkirk was called "Twinkletoes" (try hanging that on a major league player today, and see how it dances). Merrill May, another man with a florid face, was called "Pinkie." I'm sure no harm was intended, but would you want to have the nicknames assigned to Vernon Gomez (Goofy), Dick Porter (Twitchy), Alan Strange (Inky), Lloyd Brown (Gimpy), Atley Donald (Swampy), or Mel Harder (Wimpy)? Sounds like the Seven Dwarfs against Popeye the Sailor Man. Roy Mahaffey, by the way, was called "Popeye." Bill Dietrich, who wore glasses and was slightly pop-eyed, was called "Bullfrog Bill." Hazen Shirley Cuyler, who stuttered as a youth, was called "Kiki," because that was what he would say when attempting to pronounce his last name; at any odds, I'm sure he preferred that to being called Hazen Shirley. Another player, Johnny Tyler, was called "Ty Ty," but I don't know whether he had the same problem.

Bullfrog Bill Dietrich.
Right: Old Tomato Face Cullop.

Great players were more fortunate, but not immune. How would a major league star react today if you called him "Bobo," like Buck Newsome, or "Dizzy," like Jerome Dean? Johnny Murphy, an outstanding relief pitcher, was called "Grandma" and "Rocking Chair Johnny." Al Simmons was called "Bucketfoot Al"—again, calling

Ernie Lombardi hit .306 with 190 home runs in an eighteen-year career—but everyone knew him as Schnozz.

Ernie Lombardi

attention to his supposed weakness. Joe Medwick's name has been politely shortened to "Ducky" by future generations, because people today are reluctant to believe that a Hall of Famer was actually called "Ducky Wucky." But he was. Let's make up an all-star team to finish this off:

Left-handed pitcher	Gimpy
Right-handed pitcher	Wimpy
Catcher	Blimp
First base	Stinky
Second base	Inky
Third base	Pinkie
Shortstop	Rowdy Richard
Left field	Twitchy
Center field	Snooker
Right field	Ducky Wucky

TED WILLIAMS: .406 in '41

Writer Roger Angell has called Ted Williams the single best hitter he'd ever seen play baseball—and many others agree. In a nineteen-year career, interrupted for three years by World War II, Williams hit .344, with 521 home runs, a .634 slugging average, 2654 hits, and an amazing 2019 walks. In his *My Turn at Bat* (1969), with John Underwood, the Hall of Famer talks about the last days of his most famous season.

"He must have a wonderful pair of eyes," said slugger Jimmie Foxx of Ted Williams (at bat, below) in 1941. "He's got every manager in our league daffy trying to figure him out."

It was one of those years. I think, surely, to hit .400 you have to be an outstanding hitter having everything go just right, and in my case the hitter was a guy who lived to hit, who worked at it so hard he matured at the bat at a time when he was near his peak physically. The peaks met.

It was a simple formula. Choose any of the noted hitters, and none of them hit any more balls, swung a bat in practice any more times than Theodore Samuel Williams. Now, you can be a great athlete, and you can go to sleep on the bench when you should be watching the pitcher. Watch him warm up and you might pick up a clue; maybe he'll give away a pitch, or throw one he hasn't used before. You might see if he's as fast as usual, or how his curve is breaking. Pick your nose, scratch your ass and it all goes by, and you won't know enough about hitting until you're twenty-eight or twenty-nine years old, and then it'll probably be too late. . . .

It came to the last day of the season, and by now I was down to .39955, which, according to the way they do it, rounds out to an even .400. We had a doubleheader left at Philadelphia. I'd slumped as the weather got cooler, from a high of .436 in June, down to .402 in late August, then up again to .413 in September. In the last ten days of the season my average dropped almost a point a day. Now it was barely .400. The night before the game Cronin offered to take me out of the lineup to preserve the .400. They used to do that. Foxx lost a batting championship to Buddy Myer one year when he sat out the last game and Myer got two hits.

I told Cronin I didn't want that. If I couldn't hit .400 all the way I didn't deserve it. It sure as hell meant something to me then, and Johnny Orlando, the clubhouse boy, always a guy who was there when I needed him, must have walked ten miles with me the night before, talking it over and just walking around. Johnny really didn't like to walk as much as I did, so I'd wait outside while he ducked into a bar for a quick one to keep his strength up. The way he tells it, he made two stops for Scotch and I made two stops for ice cream walking the streets of Philadelphia. . . .

Now it was the last day of that 1941 season, and it turned up cold and miserable in Philadelphia. It had rained on Saturday and the game had been rescheduled as part of a Sunday doubleheader. They still had 10,000 people in Shibe Park, I suppose a lot of them just curious to see if The Kid really could hit .400. I have to say I felt good despite the cold. And I know just about everybody in the park was for me. As I came to bat for the first time that day, the Philadelphia catcher, Frankie Hayes, said, "Ted, Mr. Mack told us if we let up on you he'll run us out of baseball. I wish you all the luck in the world, but we're not giving you a damn thing."

Bill McGowan was the plate umpire, and I'll never forget it. Just as I stepped in, he called time and slowly walked around the plate, bent over and began dusting it off. Without looking up, he said, "To hit .400 a batter has got to be loose. He has got to be loose."

I guess I couldn't have been much looser. First time up I singled off Dick Fowler, a liner between first and second. Then I hit a home run, then I hit two more singles off Porter Vaughan, a left-hander who was new to me, and in the second game I hit one off the loudspeaker horn in right field for a double. For the day I wound up six for eight. I don't remember celebrating that night, but I probably went out and had a chocolate milk shake. During the winter Connie Mack had to replace the horn.

Two of the preeminent hitters of all time: Ted Williams (left) and Stan Musial.

STAN MUSIAL: "NOBODY CAN BE THAT GOOD!"

Near the end of the same season that Ted Williams hit .400, another future Hall of Famer began a career that would last twenty-two years and end with a .331 batting average, 3630 hits, 1949 runs, and 1951 RBI. From *Stan Musial* (1964), by Musial, as told to Bob Broeg.

I walked into the home clubhouse at Sportsman's Park for the first time early in the morning of September 17, 1941. With me were Erv Dusak and George Kurowski, also up from Rochester, and Walt Sessi, my old Williamson teammate reporting from Houston. The varsity hadn't arrived, but, as I was to learn through more than 20 years of pleasant association, the Cardinals' little equipment manager, Morris (Butch) Yatkeman, virtually lived there. Butch led us back to a cubbyhole where batting-practice pitchers and rookies dressed. It was called the Red-Neck Room because players who crowded into it traditionally were the unhappiest with their conditions, opportunities, salaries and, sometimes, themselves.

Stan Musial's classic coiled batting stance.

Not me. I was nervous but completely happy. . . .

My first big league manager, Billy Southworth, was a sturdy little man, a good outfielder in his day. He was deep-voiced and brisk, but he had a way with young talent. As a player, they'd called him Billy the Kid. At 48, he still looked—and acted—young. He even wore sliding pads to the coaching lines.

Southworth said he would play me at once. The Cardinals were scheduled for a doubleheader that afternoon against the seventh-place Boston Braves, managed by a seamy-faced, jug-eared man who would make his biggest mark at another time in another league—Casey Stengel. With Slaughter hurt, the Cardinals needed lefthanded hitting, so after the Redbirds had won the first game, 6–1, behind a 20-year-old lefthander, Howard Pollet, just up from Houston, I was a second-game starter.

I'll never forget facing my first big league pitcher, Jim Tobin, and the challenge of the first knuckleball I'd ever seen. It fluttered up to the plate, big as a grapefruit but dancing like a dust-devil. Offstride, fooled, I popped up weakly to Sibby Sisti, playing third base for Boston. When I trotted to right field, head down, I had a problem on my mind, a problem—and a challenge.

The knuckleball is a challenge, indeed, and I've looked foolish missing my share of knucklers. But I learned to delay my stride, cut down my swing and just stroke the ball. When I batted next against Tobin, two were on and two were out. This time I hit the ball smack against National League President Ford Frick's signature for a line drive to right-center. The ball bounced off the wall, two runs scored, and I ran joyously to second base with my first big league hit—a double.

I finished that game with two hits in four trips, the other a single, and the Cardinals won, 3–2, on a ninth-inning home run by the veteran Estel Crabtree. I was a happy kid, all right, and pretty lucky. I got a basehit the next day in a 4–1 loss to the Braves, then had my first perfect day in the majors—"3 for 3," including a double—as we beat a big Chicago righthander, Paul Erickson, 3–1.

As a result, the Cardinals were only two percentage points behind Brooklyn with nine games to play, and a crowd of more than 26,000, the most I'd every played before, came out for the Cardinals' final home games, a Sunday doubleheader with the Cubs. And at 20, a big leaguer less than a week, I enjoyed one of the finest days I'd ever have in the majors.

In the first game, playing left field, I made two good catches and threw out a runner at the plate. At bat, I doubled off the right field screen in the first inning. Next time up, I singled to center and stole second. On my third trip, I doubled off the screen again. The fourth time, with the score tied in the ninth, 5–5, I hit a one-out single for my fourth straight hit and moved to second on an infield out.

After Cubs' manager Jimmy Wilson ordered Frank Crespi passed intentionally, Coaker Triplett, swinging hard at one of lefty Ken Raffensberger's fork balls, squibbed a little grounder in front of the plate, toward third base. The Cubs' catcher, Clyde McCullough, pounced, fielded the ball and fired to Babe Dahlgren at first base. Umpire Lee Ballanfant spread his palms—"safe!"

Dahlgren whirled to argue with Ballanfant. McCullough stood watching, hands on hips. Rounding third base, I saw my chance and, without breaking stride, raced home and slid across, ahead of Dahlgren's hurried return throw to McCullough, who was scrambling back to cover home plate. I'd scored the winning run from second base on a hit that had traveled about 15 feet.

In the second game, I played right field in a 7–0 victory. I dived to my right for one low line drive and charged for another, turning a double somersault. I bunted safely toward third base and singled to center to make it a memorable six-hit day of all-round delight—for me anyway.

The Cubs' manager, Jimmy Wilson, was fit to be tied. "*Nobody*," he exploded, "can be that good!"

Stan the Man at work. "He was never colorful, never much of an interview," said Bill James. "What he was was a ballplayer."

BASEBALL AND THE WAR

With the Japanese bombing of Pearl Harbor and the entry of the United States into World War II, calls rose for major league baseball to cancel play for the duration of the war. In perhaps the most famous letter ever written by a president, Franklin Delano Roosevelt put to rest such possibilities. "I honestly feel," he wrote to Judge Landis on January 15, 1942, "that it would be best for the country to keep baseball going."

The Game Goes On

In the January 17 edition of the *Washington Post,* an edition dominated by war news and the death of film star Carole Lombard, Shirley Povich commented on the president's letter.

That man in the White House did, indeed, earn the label of the Nation's First Fan yesterday. When President Roosevelt, no less, gave the green light to organized baseball as an acceptable war-time function, the game was receiving the most extraordinary compliment of its 102-year history.

The President in declaring he saw a war-time need for the recreation provided by baseball, set at rest the fears of clubowners for their game but the clubowners and players can still butch the situation for themselves if they lose sight of Mr. Roosevelt's one injunction. It behooves them to take seriously the duty the President pointed out when he declared "individual ball players subject to service in the armed forces should carry out such obligations without question."

That means no attempts at wire-pulling, no subterfuge by star players to duck military duty with or without the support of their clubs, and no absurd claims for exemption. Such tactics would profane the very special distinction of White House blessings now bestowed on baseball, and would cause official disapproval of the game quicker than any other development. Mr. Roosevelt has put baseball on its honor, in a sense.

Thus far, however, organized baseball has merited all of Mr. Roosevelt's confidence that players will not duck their military duty. Already, it appears, more figures from the major and minor leagues have been drafted or enlisted than throughout World War I, when organized baseball's record was none too shining, with the shipyards a haven for scores of players.

To the credit of men like Clark Griffith, Tom Yawkey and Walter O. Briggs, who saw such valuable chattels as Cecil Travis, Buddy Lewis, Ted Williams, and Hank Greenberg inducted into the service, theirs was a completely patriotic reaction. "The Washington Club expects every man, star or rookie, to do his duty," said Mr. Griffith at the first hint that any of his players would be drafted, and that attitude was echoed by other clubowners.

"My Greatest Thrill"

During the four years of the war, dozens of ballplayers—stars and scrubs alike—went into the service. One was Yankee outfielder Tommy Henrich, who lost three full years of his career—but still regarded the day he left baseball for the service as his greatest day in the game. Henrich told his story to writer Fred Down in *My Greatest Baseball Game* (1950), edited by Don Schiffer.

I got my greatest thrill in baseball on August 30, 1942. It probably is the last day any one would expect me to remember as thrilling.

It started out pretty much like a thousand other Sunday afternoons in the Bronx. It was hot and humid and there was a double-header at the Yankee Stadium.

The American League race had reached a familiar point. The Yankees had all but clinched the flag and the other clubs were jockeying for first-division money. We were seven games in front and were to be eight by nightfall. This was to be our sixth pennant in seven years, a string which began in 1936, the year before I joined the club, and had been broken only in 1940 by the Detroit Tigers.

Then, as now, it was great to be a Yankee and that is why I was wearing a face a mile long when I left for the Stadium. This, you see, was to be my last day as a Yankee. By midnight I would be en route to Cleveland and the United States Coast Guard.

The crowd already was forming outside the Stadium when I arrived a little before noon. The Tigers were our guests and while they seemed out of the race they were an interesting team which always gave us a hard time.

I may have brushed past the autograph seekers rather abruptly that day. I'm sorry if I did. But baseball and autographs seemed so far away and the war so close. I was to learn more about those fans later.

In the clubhouse it was the same as usual. Red Ruffing, who was to work the first game, was sitting in front of his locker reading a magazine. There were the usual chatter and jokes. I tried to look casual.

"Hey Schulte," I said to Coach John Schulte who minded the ball bag. "Give me a mess of balls, will you?"

"All you want," he said. "Today you get all you want."

But he already was leaving the clubhouse for the field and I knew he wouldn't be an easy touch. He never was.

I don't remember too much about the first game. Ruffing was no longer a 20-game winner but he knew how to pitch and he was always very effective against the Tigers. He worked fast and the Tigers never did get him into serious trouble. We won, going away, 8 to 1. I got three hits.

They threw Dizzy Trout against us in the second game and I guess you know what kind of a pitcher he was. He hadn't become a consistent winner yet but he was a big, strong guy with a lot of stuff. He could be tough when he was "on" and he always seemed to be "on" when he worked against us. I believe he is one of three or four American League pitchers who holds an edge over the Yankees for his career.

We got a run early but the Tigers hung in there and it was 3 to 2 our favor at the end of six innings. I didn't like it. One bad pitch and the Tigers could tie it up. We needed another run and I figured Trout wasn't going to get himself into serious trouble. I figured we needed to get that run with one swing and the "homer" was uppermost in my mind when my turn came to hit in the seventh.

"This could be my last swing as a Yankee," I said to myself as I left the dugout for the batter's circle. "It would be good to go out with a homer."

Then it was my turn and I threw aside the extra bats I'd been swinging and started for the plate.

"Attention, please. . . . Attention, please. . . ."

It was the public address system and I'll never forget the announcer's voice—hard and metallic.

"This one's not even over and there's the announcement for tomorrow's game," I said under my breath. "You'd think he could wait until we had this one won."

". . . Ladies and gentlemen," the voice went on, *"this is the last appearance of Tommy Henrich in a Yankee uniform until the war is over."*

Opposite: Tommy Henrich, for one day, at least, the Yankees' greatest star.

"O.K.," I thought, "so what if I don't hit?"

The rumble in the stands—the exact count I learned later was 50,398—seemed to start in the bleachers. But within seconds it had become the loudest roar I'd ever heard.

I tipped my cap and looked up into the stands. Everybody was standing. I kicked at the dirt and waited. The roar went on. I tipped my cap again. Still it went on. I looked out at the mound. Trout was standing there laughing. He must have known how I felt. And I knew he was thinking I'd be easy meat when I finally got into the batter's box.

"Come on, you big lug," I yelled. "Pitch! Let's get this thing over with."

He turned his back and picked up the resin bag. He was still laughing when he looked around again. The roar from the stands was as loud as ever. I wished it would stop. I never felt so helpless in my life.

"Come on, Trout," I yelled again. "Throw!"

Now Trout was about halfway from the mound to the plate and he had stopped laughing.

"What are you in such a rush about?" he yelled. "This is for you and you'll never hear anything like it again. You couldn't buy what you're getting now, so stand there and take it."

He was right, of course. I know that now. You hit a homer—win a game—maybe win a World Series game and you remember them as great thrills. But they're nothing compared to having 50,000 people you don't even know standing and giving you a send-off like I received.

No, I didn't hit that homer although the Yankees did win. The best I could do was a single—a grounder through the box. But I didn't care. I already had had my greatest thrill in baseball.

Hank Greenberg's War

While many players served in noncombat capacities, some saw battle action. Hall of Famer Hank Greenberg was one of the first stars to enlist (actually, he re-enlisted after Pearl Harbor, having already fulfilled his military duty). Greenberg lost almost four full seasons to the war, leaving for the service just one home run short of 250 for his career—a round-tripper he finally hit in 1945, soon after his return. In this article by Arthur Daley in the February 14, 1945, *New York Times*, Greenberg discusses his wartime exploits.

*Hank Greenberg and
Joe DiMaggio go to war.*

Captain Hank has had almost four years in which to think about that 250th homer he never made. And he has had almost four years to wonder whether he'll ever make it or will be too old to return as a player when he is finally mustered out of service. He's wondered about it in all sorts of strange places, including an airplane while flying over the dreaded hump from India into China.

"I must confess, though," he remarked, "that I hardly gave it full consideration then. Flying the Hump is a pretty nerve-racking experience. I went over it five times and you're always worried about the weather. It's rare that you have a clear day. If you fly over the weather, you're sweating it out in fear you won't be able to find your landing field when you come down through it. If you fly through the weather, you're constantly afraid you'll hit one of those mountain peaks.

Hammerin' Hank, at his other job.

"Always in the back of your mind is the fact that if anything goes wrong the plane can't be landed. I got a good look at that country on the only clear flying day I had. It's an awe-inspiring yet terrifying view. I could see Mount Everest a hundred or so miles away. That rugged scenery was desolate but breath-taking."

Hank stared off into space as memories of the Himalayas flooded back into his mind. "I'll never forget the first mission our B-29's made from our base to Japan," he said. "I drove out to the field in a jeep with Gen. Blondy Saunders, who led the strike, and took my place in the control tower. Those monsters went off, one after the other, with clocklike precision.

"Then we spotted one fellow in trouble. The pilot saw he wasn't going to clear the runway, tried to throttle down, but the plane went over on its nose at the end of the field. Father Stack, our padre, and myself raced over to the burning ship to see if we could help rescue anyone. As we were running there was a blast when the gas tanks blew up and we were only about thirty yards away when a bomb went off. It knocked us right into a drainage ditch alongside the rice paddies while pieces of metal floated down out of the air.

"I was stunned and couldn't talk or hear for a couple of days, but was otherwise undamaged. The miraculous part of it all, however, was that the entire crew escaped. Some of them were pretty well banged up but no one was killed. That also was an occasion, I can assure you, when I didn't wonder whether or not I'd be able to return to baseball. I was quite satisfied just to be alive."

PART FOUR

1946–1975: YEARS OF PEACE

"Peace on earth means more resonance in the cry of 'Play ball!'" wrote Herbert Simons in the October 1945 *Baseball Magazine*. "It means boom crowds . . . the return of scores of big-name stars . . . the glamour again of the DiMaggios, the Williamses, the Fellers. . . . It means, in fact, that post-war baseball, like many another cherished commodity, will be pre-war plus."

Simons knew whereof he wrote. In 1945, when it was becoming clear that the war would finally end, attendance at major league games set a new record of 10.8 million. In 1946, the first postwar season, attendance exploded to 18.5 million—by far the greatest gain ever in one year.

Cleveland's Bob Feller, one of the biggest stars of the postwar period.

Yet while fans flooded the parks to see a "pre-war plus" game, what they got was actually very different. One important change was the advent, at last, of widespread night baseball. When such holdouts as the Yankees and Tigers finally accepted the inevitable and installed lights, baseball quickly discovered what now seems obvious: Many more people are able to attend games at night than ever could during the day.

But the greatest change in the game—a seismic shift—didn't occur until 1947. This, of course, was the arrival of Jackie Robinson, the first ballplayer to break the decades-old color barrier. At last Robinson and those who soon followed—Larry Doby, Roy Campanella, Monte Irvin, Ernie Banks, Don Newcombe, Willie Mays, Henry Aaron, and other stars—got the chance to prove they belonged in the majors—and prove it they did. Along with increased numbers of Latin stars, including Minnie Minoso and, later, Roberto Clemente, Luis Aparicio, the Alou brothers, and Juan Marichal, the black players allowed baseball to reflect the diversity of the country whose national game it was.

Ironically, while the face of baseball had never been more varied, the game itself was gradually becoming far less adventurous. "In the early part of the 1950s," Bill James points out, "every team approached the game with the same essential offensive philosophy: get people on base and hit home runs."

The preponderance of power hitters caused the stolen base, hit-and-run, and other strategies relying on speed to fall into disuse. Teams rarely stole more than seventy-five bases a season. Willie Mays, who came up in 1951, led all players in stolen bases for the decade with 179—an average of less than twenty per year, and about the total reached by today's speed merchants in three seasons.

Minnie Minoso, the first of the great Latin players who entered the majors after Jackie Robinson breached the color barrier, beating the throw home.

The early and mid-1950s were a wonderful time to be a fan—if you happened to live in New York. During these years, the Giants, Dodgers, and Yankees played ping-pong with the pennant, capturing fifteen of the twenty flags won during the decade. Unsurprisingly, what many believe was the greatest game ever played—the 1951 playoff capped by Bobby Thomson's famous home run off Ralph Branca—was a contest between the Giants and Dodgers for the right to play the Yankees in the World Series.

If the three teams were baseball's royalty, the Yankees were clearly king. From 1947 to 1957, the years Roger Kahn has dubbed "the Era," the Bronx Bombers alone won seven World Series. No wonder Mickey Mantle, Yogi Berra, Phil Rizzuto, Whitey Ford, and a slew of other Yankee stars left more indelible impressions than the great players—including Eddie Matthews, Stan Musial, Early Wynn, and others—who toiled for less successful teams.

Perhaps not coincidentally, baseball overall suffered serious attendance problems in the early 1950s. After reaching more than twenty million in 1948, attendance at major league games dropped steadily, with six million fewer fans attending games by 1953.

Phil Rizzuto guns one over to first during the 1949 Yankee-Dodger World Series—a typical clutch play for both the dominant Yankee teams of the time and the 1994 electee to the Hall of Fame.

Overleaf: Eddie Stanky and Jackie Robinson in one of the many tense moments that characterized Giant-Dodger clashes.

Whitey Ford, the Yanks' best pitcher during "the Era."

Television was considered the main culprit. While in 1951, *Baseball Magazine* had editorialized that "Games Must Be Televised," a year later the same magazine said that "TV Must Go . . . Or Baseball Will." This change in sentiment reflected the widespread perception that fans wouldn't bother going to the ballpark if they could watch the games at home.

One perhaps inevitable result of the attendance slump was the spate of franchise shifts that occurred throughout the fifties. The Boston Braves moved to Milwaukee in '53, the St. Louis Browns to Baltimore in '54, and the Philadelphia Athletics to Kansas City in '55. The epidemic peaked, of course, in 1958, when the Brooklyn Dodgers and New York Giants fled to Los Angeles and San Francisco, respectively—a decision still seen as an unpardonable betrayal by countless fans.

Still, out of these shaky times a new, more exciting brand of baseball began to emerge. By the early 1960s, speed had resumed a more prominent place in the game, led by Maury Wills's 104 stolen bases in 1962. With expansion's addition of two teams to each league, batting averages grew healthier, with more home runs being hit than ever before.

Then, in seeming rebuke to reawakened offenses, the Baseball Rules Committee chose to enlarge the strike zone after the '62 season. In conjunction with the arrival of new, more spacious stadiums, this change ushered in a dramatic era of the pitcher.

Today, it's hard to imagine the extent to which power pitchers dominated the game through 1968. While familiar sluggers—Willie Mays and Hank Aaron—and newer stars—Willie McCovey and Frank Robinson—still put up good batting numbers, the pitchers—Sandy Koufax, Bob Gibson, Juan Marichal, Don Drysdale, and many others—thrived on the new conditions. Strikeouts, shutouts, no-hit games, and other signs of the pitchers' domination reached levels rarely seen before.

The peak (or nadir) of this trend occurred in 1968, which Roger Angell has dubbed "The Year of the Infield Pop-Up." The entire American League batted just .230, and Carl Yastrzemski won the batting title with a .301 mark—less than the National League as a whole batted in 1930. Conversely, the Red Sox's Luis Tiant led the league with a minuscule 1.60 ERA, while Tommy John's 1.98 ERA for the White Sox was good enough for only fifth best in the league.

The Yankees' brilliant manager Casey Stengel: Glinty eyes, a big nose, and (as Baseball Magazine *put it), "awesome ears of about the same size, shape and constituency of rib lamb chops."*

Opposite: Speedster Maury Wills swiping his then-record 104th base in 1962.

Frank Robinson, the first
African-American major league
manager, with commissioner
Bowie Kuhn in 1975.

Not that the N.L. was much stronger offensively. This was the year, for example, that Bob Gibson boasted an ERA of 1.12, completed twenty-eight games, threw thirteen shutouts, and still managed to lose nine times.

These aberrant numbers forced the league magnates to make some hurried redress. For the 1969 season, the strike zone was shrunk again, and the pitcher's mound was lowered. Other changes, such as improving visibility for the hitters and the institution of the designated hitter in the A.L. in 1973, also helped restore the balance between pitcher and batter.

Of course Gibson, Steve Carlton, Jim Palmer, Tom Seaver, and other pitchers continued to post great stats. But by 1971 the A.L. batting championship was won by Minnesota's Tony Oliva with a healthy .337, while the Cardinals' Joe Torre blasted to a .363 mark in the N.L. Meanwhile, the early seventies featured sluggers like Willie Stargell, Hank Aaron, Johnny Bench, Bobby Bonds, and Reggie Jackson who routinely hit thirty or more home runs, while Lou Brock, Joe Morgan, Bert Campaneris, and Davey Lopes were stealing fifty, sixty, even seventy bases a season—or, in the case of Brock in 1974, a remarkable 118 bases, two-thirds the total Willie Mays achieved in the entire decade of the fifties.

Unsurprisingly, attendance recovered nicely from the malaise that had begun in the fifties. One reason for the leap forward may have been the institution of divisional play in 1969, which doubled the potential number of pennant races in each league. The D.H. also undoubtedly improved A.L. attendance.

But mostly fans came back because the game had again become entertaining. In addition to a slew of multitalented players, an array of colorful teams came and went during these years. The '69 Miracle Mets, the arrogant Oakland A's, winners of three consecutive World Series in 1972–74, the Big Red Machine of the early and mid-seventies—these were teams with personality, teams to love or hate wholeheartedly. Perhaps even more importantly, none was as dominating, as unshakable, as the Yankee dynasty had been from the late forties through the mid-sixties. No matter what team you rooted for, you could at least hope that it might be in line to win the Series, if not this year then next.

Perhaps the finest moment of the entire era took place at its very end: The 1975 World Series. This breathless seven-game affair, culminating in seesaw battles in the last two games ("perhaps the most exciting 24 hours in all of sports history," wrote David Nemec in *The Ultimate Baseball Book*), seemed to announce once and for all that baseball was back as the nation's favorite sport.

Cincinnati manager Sparky Anderson and catcher Johnny Bench celebrate the Reds' victory in the '75 World Series—one of the best Series of all time.

The same season also witnessed another breakthrough: The appointment of Frank Robinson as manager of the Cleveland Indians. Robinson, the first African-American to manage a major league team, paved the way for those who followed, though for a long time he was the only nonwhite to manage more than a handful of games in the majors. Not until 1993, in fact, could the majors boast an adequate number of black and Latin managers, including the world champion Toronto Blue Jays' skipper Cito Gaston, the San Francisco Giants' Dusty Baker, the Kansas City Royals' Hal McRae, the Montreal Expos' Felipe Alou, and the Colorado Rockies' Don Baylor.

But if fan enthusiasm, brilliant on-field play, and greater diversification seemed to revitalize the game in '75, that year also marked the last season before a sea change that would alter baseball forever. The Players Association, under the leadership of Marvin Miller, had been marshaling its energy for several years, and in 1975 it fired the shot that would be heard throughout the game: Two pitchers, Andy Messersmith and Dave McNally, sued baseball in an attempt to overturn the reserve clause, the rule that tied players to a specific team in perpetuity. The pitchers thought this was unfair. They wanted to be free agents.

1947: A BARRIER FINALLY FALLS

No event in baseball history has had a greater impact on the game than the arrival of Jackie Robinson on the Brooklyn Dodgers in 1947. The story of Robinson's strength, of how he overcame the often vicious prejudice he faced to fashion a Hall of Fame career, has been often told by historians. In the following excerpts, however, the men who were actually there—Dodgers' owner Branch Rickey, who brought Robinson to the team, pitcher Kirby Higbe, manager Leo Durocher, and Robinson himself—create a portrait of a time and a process that are almost incomprehensible to a fan watching baseball today.

Rickey had long hoped to be the first man to integrate baseball. Stymied by Judge Landis, who refused to consider the possibility of allowing a nonwhite ballplayer to reach the majors, Rickey tried again after Landis's death in 1945— and found a far more sympathetic ear in new commissioner A. B. "Happy" Chandler.

"How Could a Man of Worth and Human Dignity Bend Enough?"

Once he'd been given the go-ahead, as Rickey recounted in his 1965 book, *The American Diamond,* he faced a new challenge: Picking the right individual to serve as the first man to cross the color barrier.

Branch Rickey (right) on Jackie Robinson: "It took an intelligent man to understand the challenge—it took a man of great moral courage to accept it and see it through. He was both."

Opposite: Jackie Robinson as a rookie first baseman, 1947.

One of the most worrying of all problems was finding the man who would be all right off the field. We could know about his playing ability in uniform—but what about out of uniform? Could he take it? What about his habits, his associates, his character, his education, his intelligence? Could the man handle his own people? Could he handle himself? What about transportation, hotels? What about the Jim Crow customs? Could he be fully and wisely cooperative in avoiding race adulation—gifts, dinners, awards, etc.? How could he oppose mass or group attendances of his own race?

How could a man of worth and human dignity bend enough? How could a man with a distinctive personality keep it untarnished with constant absorption of attacks calculated to destroy his self-respect? There just are not very many such humans. The trial candidate must never lose his sense of purpose nor lower his sights from the ultimate goal of making good off the field.

I had employed scouts in Puerto Rico, Cuba, and Mexico for over a year, only finally to find out that the best Negro players were in our own United States. One of the names on the list was Jackie Robinson. The scouting of the player was begun by Wendell Smith, a Negro writer for the *Pittsburgh Courier.* Then Wid Mathews followed up on him, followed by George Sisler and finally by Clyde Sukeforth. All these men believed they were scouting for the Brooklyn Brown Dodgers. Other than the reports of these very able experts, I knew nothing about the Negro player who was recommended. I simply accepted the judgment of my scouts.

Here was a boy who lacked a few hours' credit to a degree from UCLA. He had been a fine football player and a basketball and track star—less known in baseball than in any other major sport. He enlisted in the U.S. armed services as a private. He came out an officer. If direction determines value, Robinson was on his way.

Clyde Sukeforth brought Jackie to Brooklyn for an interview. This was the first time I had ever met him. Both Sukeforth and Robinson believed that he was to be offered a contract with the Brooklyn Brown Dodgers, a colored team. It was hard to convince the player that he was facing a job in the major leagues. At the end of a three-hour conference, Robinson showed the necessary intelligence and the strength of personality, but he had more and deeper racial resentment than was hoped for or expected. I tested and probed with many questions. If he were subjected to the very lowest depth of scurrility involving him and his own mother—"What would you do?"

"I'd kill him" showed the exact strength that was needed. But how could I bandage it and keep it fully alive?

An Uprising Planned

Having convinced himself that Robinson could handle the inevitable abuse from opposing teams—could, in fact, stifle his pride and turn the other cheek—Rickey signed him to the Dodgers. After a year starring with the team's minor league affiliate in Montreal, Robinson joined the big club in the spring of 1947 and accompanied them on a Latin America tour. "A poll of the players would run heavily against the dusky Montreal farmhand," said the *Brooklyn Eagle* after Robinson joined the team, "but Jackie has a way of winning friends and influencing people and might win over the Dodgers." As Kirby Higbe recounts in his honest autobiography, *The High Hard One* (with Martin Quigley, 1967), the newspaper's cautious optimism was misplaced.

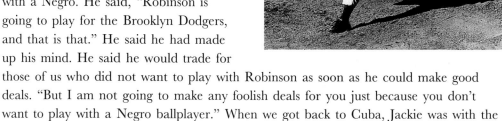

There were five of us that went straight to Mr. Rickey. All of us were Southerners—Pee Wee Reese, Dixie Walker, Bobby Bragan, and me—except Carl Furillo, who was from Pennsylvania. We told Mr. Rickey that we did not want to play ball with a Negro. He said, "Robinson is going to play for the Brooklyn Dodgers, and that is that." He said he had made up his mind. He said he would trade for those of us who did not want to play with Robinson as soon as he could make good deals. "But I am not going to make any foolish deals for you just because you don't want to play with a Negro ballplayer." When we got back to Cuba, Jackie was with the ball club.

Pee Wee and I had an apartment together that spring, but Leo was staying at the Nacional Hotel and was married at that time to Laraine Day. He and Laraine invited Pee Wee and me to have dinner with them one night to talk to us about playing with Jackie. Leo said that he had heard that Mr. Rickey was going to trade us away as soon as he could make good deals, but that as long as he was manager of the club we would never be traded. He told us what a great player Jackie was and how he could help us win the pennant. Laraine told us what a great guy he was, a nice quiet fellow that we wouldn't have to associate with off the field. We talked for a couple of hours, but they didn't change our minds.

We didn't have anything personal against Jackie Robinson or any other Negro. As Southerners who had played ball up North for several years, we had heard a lot of talk about how we abused and mistreated Negroes down South, and we knew we never had. We had never had any race riots or trouble with Negroes in my neck of the woods down South, but I had seen and heard of plenty of trouble in Detroit, New York, and St. Louis.

We had several more talks with Leo and Laraine about it, but we were Southerners who had never lived or played with Negroes, and we didn't see any reason to start then.

Never afraid to speak his mind, Leo Durocher was one of Robinson's strongest supporters.

Opposite: Dodger pitcher Kirby Higbe, who claimed he didn't have anything personal against Robinson.

An Uprising Put Down

Durocher, in his autobiography, *Nice Guys Finish Last* (with Ed Linn, 1975), continues the story.

Mr. Rickey had some kind of pipe dream that as soon as the players recognized how much Jackie could help us, they were going to demand that he be brought up.

What happened was exactly the opposite. Early in the spring we went to Panama for a weekend series against a squad of Caribbean All-Stars. The Montreal club, including Robinson and three other Negro players—Roy Campanella, Don Newcombe and Roy Partlow—came to Panama too. The Dodgers stayed at the U.S. army barracks at Fort Gulick. The Montreal players had their own quarters on the other side of the Isthmus.

We had been there about a week when one of my coaches, Clyde Sukeforth, reported he was picking up talk that the players, led by Dixie Walker and Eddie Stanky, were getting up a petition to warn us that they would never play with Robinson.

I had seen Robinson in a couple of the Montreal exhibition games, and that was all it took to convince me that I wanted him. He was still playing second base with Montreal—he wasn't handed a first-baseman's mitt until the season was about to start—and you could see how he could move in the field and could run the bases. But most of all, you could see he was a really good hitter. And that nothing in the world scared him.

Since Mr. Rickey was due to join us in a couple of days, I decided to hold off and let him handle it. I was not completely convinced, understand, that the story was true. What did the damn fools think they were going to do—strike? To check it out, I spent the day testing some of the players. I'd turn the conversation around to Jackie Robinson and say, "Doesn't bother me any . . ." or "If this kid can play ball, boy, I want him on the ball club. . . ." The reactions, though somewhat guarded, were far from encouraging. The rumors were true all right.

As I lay in bed that night, unable to sleep, I suddenly asked myself why I was being so cute about it. Hell, I was getting as bad as Rickey. The thing to do, I could see, was to nip it in the bud, step on them hard before they had taken the irretrievable step of signing the petition and presenting it to anybody. Once the battle lines were drawn, it was going to become a very messy situation. And while they couldn't possibly win, the club couldn't possibly come out of it without being ripped apart, either. I made up my mind right there that there was going to be no petition. Not if I had anything to say about it.

I jumped right out of bed, woke up my coaches and instructed them to round up all the players and bring them downstairs. Still in my pajamas, I scouted around for a meeting place and stumbled across the perfect place. A huge, empty kitchen right behind the mess hall.

In came the players, some in pajamas, some in their underwear, some buckling their trousers. They sat on the chopping blocks and on the counters; they leaned sleepily against the refrigerator and the stoves.

I said: "I hear some of you fellows don't want to play with Robinson and that you have a petition drawn up that you are going to sign. Well, boys, you know what you can do with that petition. You can wipe your ass with it. Mr. Rickey is on his way down here and all you have to do is tell him about it. I'm sure he'll be happy to make other arrangements for you.

"I hear Dixie Walker is going to send Mr. Rickey a letter asking to be traded. Just hand him the letter, Dixie, and you're gone. Gone! If this fellow is good enough to play on this ball club—and from what I've seen and heard, he is—he is going to play on this ball club and he is going to play for me."

I said: "I'm the manager of this ball club, and I'm interested in one thing. Winning. I'll play an elephant if he can do the job, and to make room for him I'll send my own brother home. So make up your mind to it. This fellow is a real great ballplayer. He's going to win pennants for us. He's going to put money in your pockets and money in mine. And here's something else to think about when you put your head back on the pillow. From everything I hear, he's only the first. Only the first, boys! There's many more coming right behind him and they have the talent and they're gonna come to play. These fellows are hungry. They're good athletes and there's nowhere else they can make this kind of money. They're going to come, boys, and they're going to come scratching and diving. Unless you fellows look out and wake up, they're going to run you right out of the ball park.

"So," I said, "I don't want to see your petition and I don't want to hear anything more about it. The meeting is over; go back to bed."

"I Gritted My Teeth"

In an obscure 1948 autobiography, *Jackie Robinson: My Own Story* (as told to Wendell Smith), Robinson tried to be conciliatory. But some of his anger and frustration unavoidably came through.

The one thing my wife kept cautioning me about was my temper. I had the reputation on the West Coast of being an athlete with a quick temper. They said I had a habit of flaring up and fighting back if necessary. Usually that is regarded as a good trait in an

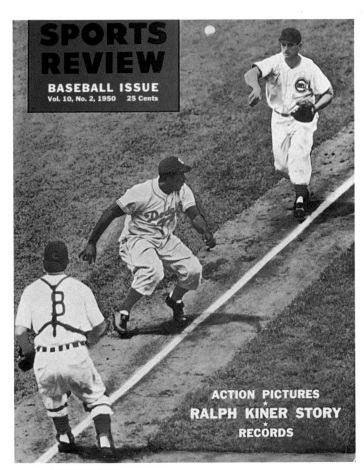

Robinson's aggressiveness on the basepaths made an impact on every game he played in.

athlete. It means that the fellow is a fighter and game to the core. College coaches like men like that. I think I did fight to win as hard as the other boys on our UCLA teams and on the other teams we played, but I don't think I was ever a "sore-head" or a trouble-maker. Many things of which I had been accused were simply untrue.

I knew, however, that I would have to live down my reputation—no matter how unjustified—from the moment I arrived in training camp. Because I was a Negro, I knew I had to remain calm all the time. My wife also knew it, and she kept drilling the admonition into my mind. I guess she half-believed I was hotheaded, because she had been present several times when I had encountered discrimination and had seen me get so angry that I had almost blown up. These occasions had produced whispers: "That Jackie Robinson may be a good athlete, but he has a bad temper." The whispers were so consistent and far-flung that they had reached Brooklyn. I learned, in fact, that Branch Rickey was more than a little concerned over this alleged characteristic of mine. He had said that he was going to try to "harness" me, but that if he couldn't, he would give me my release. That made me realize what a great risk he had taken in signing me. If I didn't keep my temper, I would embarrass not only him, but thousands of other people who were pulling for me to make good.

On the way to the airport, I listened to my wife. I made up my mind that I was going to disprove that "bad temper" propaganda. The rumor had begun when I was in college. In the heat of games, any athlete will scream "murder" sometimes, and I was no exception. If a UCLA player got roughed-up in a football game, for instance, I was right in the middle of any ruckus that developed. Maybe I was a bit too aggressive in those days. After all, I was a Negro, and the pattern of conduct for Negroes in almost any relation with white people has been, if not a subservient attitude, at least one of keeping quiet and remaining in the background. I don't think I was more aggressive than the other players, but I guess people were just not used to seeing a Negro heatedly "talking back" to white men in the very middle of a stadium jammed with thousands of people. . . .

The first racial "incident" occurred in April, when the Phillies came to Brooklyn for a three-game series. The Phillies, led by their very able manager, Ben Chapman, are great bench-riders. The first time I stepped up to the plate, they opened up full blast. "Hey, you black Nigger," I heard one of them yell. "Why don't you go back where you came from?" Then I heard another one shout: "Yeah, pretty soon you'll want to eat and sleep with white ball players!" As the jockeying continued on this level, I almost lost my head. I started to drop my bat and go over and take a sock at one of them. But then I remembered Branch Rickey's warning me of what I'd have to take without losing my temper. So I pretended I didn't hear them. I gritted my teeth and vented some of my anger on a solid single.

"You know if I had been pitching to Ruth and Gehrig, you could knock a few points off those big fat lifetime batting averages," said Satchel Paige (right).

Opposite: Jackie Robinson's fiery style encapsulated in a single play: A daring steal of home against Yogi Berra and the Yankees in the 1955 World Series.

THOSE WHO DIDN'T MAKE IT

Unfortunately, while the game on the field allowed Robinson some refuge from the intense pressure, the wounds left by racism lasted the rest of his life. Roger Angell, who had witnessed Robinson completely lose control of his temper, for no apparent reason, during a game in the 1950s, wrote: "After that moment, I knew that we had asked him to do too much for us. None of it—probably not a day of it—was ever easy for him."

Other African-American ballplayers, at least Robinson's equal in talent, suffered just as greatly from baseball's institutionalized prejudice. A few, including the magnificent pitcher Satchel Paige, at least had a taste of the majors, but many others, including Hall of Famer Josh Gibson, missed their chance. The Giants' star outfielder Monte Irvin, also a veteran of the Negro Leagues, paid tribute to some of them in Anthony J. Connor's *Baseball for the Love of It* (1982).

> The only comparison I can give is—suppose Willie Mays had never had a chance to play big league. Then I were to come to you and try to tell you about Willie Mays. Now this is the way it is with Cool Papa Bell. This is the way it is with Buck Leonard. Just a fantastic hitter. With Oscar Charleston, who they say was just as good as Willie— or *better*. But very few people ever saw him play.

Monte Irvin (above), one of many Negro League stars who made it to home plate in the majors only because Jackie Robinson (right) went there first.

There were others. I'm thinking about John Beckwith. Ray Dandridge, third baseman. Willie Wells, shortstop. Sammy T. Hughes, second baseman. Leon Day, who was a pitcher just like Bob Gibson. And on and on. I'm thinking about Smokey Joe Williams and Mule Suttles and Biz Mackey, and right on down the line.

If they could have removed the Jim Crow barrier even just ten years earlier, there would've been twenty to twenty-five men they could've taken right onto major league clubs as regulars and they'd have been potential Hall of Famers. There were *that* many.

So Jackie Robinson was *not* the best. He was just the first. And a very fine choice as it turned out. What made Jackie so outstanding was his personal color and his competitive fire. He wasn't a good hitter at the beginning, but he *made* himself into one. He had great natural speed and quickness and used it to full advantage. He *made* himself into an all-star second baseman, and he developed the knack of stealing bases and particularly stealing home. He'd drive pitchers *crazy* and he was very thrilling to watch. So he drew fans to the park and sparked his team to victory and, as I said, turned out to be an excellent choice for the pioneering role. Not many people could've controlled themselves so well in the face of all that pressure and abuse.

Later, after he didn't have to be a pioneer anymore and could let himself fight back, we all saw what kind of fires Jackie really had burning inside.

For some Negro Leaguers, including Cool Papa Bell (here, sliding into third), the color barrier was lifted too late.

HANK GREENBERG: SPEAKING FROM EXPERIENCE

Jackie Robinson and other nonwhite ballplayers were not the only ones to experience prejudice. In this 1949 letter to a Philadelphia doctor, recently retired slugger Hank Greenberg expressed a philosophy developed after many difficult experiences as a highly visible figure in a profession that featured very few Jews.

Dear Doctor:

In reply to your letter requesting advice for the young baseball player you refer to, I suggest that you tell him to concentrate on his playing and forget about all outside influences.

Baseball is a game that affords any youngster an opportunity to progress. Ability is the sole determining factor in advancement, and not religion, the way your hair parts or your parental lineage.

I speak from experience. I started from the bottom and worked myself up to the top. Sure, I was confronted with many difficulties, many obstacles and could have easily called it quits and blamed my failure on prejudice. Many baseball failures feel that their lack of success is primarily due to the fact that they are Catholics, Protestants or do not come from the social register. I am certain that the youngster you refer to will reach the big leagues if he has the necessary physical and mental ability. Every Major League Club is searching desperately for talent. Hundreds of thousands of dollars are being spent to uncover Major League talent and no one cares whether the player is a Hindu, a Chinaman or a Jew.

Please convey this advice to your young friend. If time permitted I would go into this subject more thoroughly, but I am sure that you and your friend know what I am driving at.

Very truly yours,
"Hank" Greenberg

P.S. If prejudice does exist and I refuse to recognize that it does, then let it spur you on to greater achievement rather than accept it and be licked by it.

JOE DIMAGGIO, YOUNG OLD MASTER

The image of Joe DiMaggio is so deeply engrained in the minds of fans that his actual accomplishments seem hazy. In a thirteen-year career interrupted for three seasons by World War II, though, Joe D hit below .300 only twice, slammed thirty or more home runs seven times, compiled a .579 slugging average (sixth best of all time)—and fielded and ran the bases with incomparable self-confidence and grace. In "Young Old Master" (first published in the January 8, 1948, *New York Herald-Tribune,* reprinted in *Out of the Red,* 1950), Red Smith pays tribute to the great Yankee star.

After the Yankees chewed up the Dodgers in the second game of the World Series, Joe DiMaggio relaxed in the home club's gleaming tile boudoir and deposed at length in defense of Pete Reiser, the Brooklyn center fielder, who had narrowly escaped being smitten upon the isthmus rhombencephali that day by sundry fly balls.

The moving, mottled background of faces and shirt collars and orchids, Joe said, made a fly almost invisible until it had cleared the top deck. The tricky, slanting shadows of an October afternoon created a problem involving calculus, metaphysics, and social hygiene when it came to judging a line drive. The roar of the crowd disguised the crack of bat against ball. And so on.

Our Mr. Robert Cooke, listening respectfully as one should to the greatest living authority on the subject, nevertheless stared curiously at DiMaggio. He was thinking that not only Reiser but also J. DiMaggio had played that same center field on that same afternoon, and there were no knots on Joe's slick coiffure.

"How about you, Joe?" Bob asked. "Do those same factors handicap you out there?"

DiMaggio permitted himself one of his shy, toothy smiles.

"Don't start worrying about the old boy after all these years," he said.

He didn't say "the old master." That's a phrase for others to use. But it would be difficult to define more aptly than Joe did the difference between this unmitigated pro and all the others, good, bad, and ordinary, who also play in major-league outfields.

There is a line that has been quoted so often the name of its originator has been lost. But whoever said it first was merely reacting impulsively to a particular play and not trying to coin a mot when he ejaculated: "The sonofagun! Ten years I've been watching him, and he hasn't had a hard chance yet!"

It may be that Joe is not, ranked on his defensive skill alone, the finest center fielder of his time. Possibly Terry Moore was his equal playing the hitter, getting the jump on the ball, judging a fly, covering ground, and squeezing the ball once he touched it.

Joe himself has declared that his kid brother, Dominic, is a better fielder than he. Which always recalls the occasion when the Red Sox were playing the Yanks and Dom fled across the county

The effortlessly graceful Joe DiMaggio.

"He simply had no weaknesses," said Bob Feller of DiMaggio, a baserunner who is remembered for never making a mistake.

line to grab a drive by Joe that no one but a DiMaggio could have reached. And the late Sid Mercer, shading his thoughtful eyes under a hard straw hat, remarked to the press box at large: "Joe should sue his old man on that one."

Joe hasn't been the greatest hitter that baseball has known, either. He'll not match Ty Cobb's lifetime average, he'll never threaten Babe Ruth's home-run record, nor will he ever grip the imagination of the crowds as the Babe did. Or even as Babe Herman did. That explains why the contract that he signed the other day calls for an estimated $65,000 instead of the $80,000 that Ruth got. If he were not such a matchless craftsman he might be a more spectacular player. And so, perhaps, more colorful. And so more highly rewarded.

But you don't rate a great ballplayer according to his separate, special talents. You must rank him off the sum total of his component parts, and on this basis there has not been, during Joe's big-league existence, a rival close to him. None other in his time has combined such savvy and fielding and hitting and throwing—Tom Laird, who was

writing sports in San Francisco when Joe was growing up, always insisted that a sore arm "ruined" DiMaggio's throwing in his first season with the Yankees—and such temperament and such base running.

Because he does so many other things so well and makes no specialty of stealing, DiMaggio rarely has received full credit for his work on the bases. But travel with a second-division club in the league for a few seasons and count the times when DiMaggio, representing the tying or winning run, whips you by coming home on the unforeseen gamble and either beats the play or knocks the catcher into the dugout.

Ask American League catchers about him, or National Leaguers like Ernie Lombardi. Big Lom will remember who it was who ran home from first base in the last game of the 1939 World Series while Ernie lay threshing in the dust behind the plate and Bucky Walters stood bemused on the mound.

These are the reasons why DiMaggio, excelled by Ted Williams in all offensive statistics and reputedly Ted's inferior in crowd appeal and financial standing, still won the writers' accolade as the American League's most valuable in 1947.

It wasn't the first time Williams earned this award with his bat and lost it with his disposition. As a matter of fact, if all other factors were equal save only the question of character, Joe never would lose out to any player. The guy who came out of San Francisco as a shy lone wolf, suspicious of Easterners and of Eastern writers, today is the top guy in any sports gathering in any town. The real champ.

Joe DiMaggio: "Baseball was my life. It was all I ever wanted to know."

WILLIE MAYS OPENS SOME EYES

Everyone who ever watched Willie Mays play remembers the sheer joy Mays brought to every game—the ebullience that seemed to carry him to his Hall of Fame achievements: 660 home runs (trailing just Aaron and Ruth), 1903 RBI, 3283 hits. But for many, the deepest pleasure in watching Mays came from seeing him in the field, racing out from under his cap as he tracked down yet another seemingly uncatchable fly ball. In *Day with the Giants* (1952), edited by Kyle Crichton, actress Laraine Day—star of Alfred Hitchcock's *Foreign Correspondent* and other films, and married at the time to Giants manager Leo Durocher—recalls the first time she began to understand just how good Mays was.

Giants' manager Leo Durocher and his wife, actress Laraine Day, couldn't take their eyes off the young Willie Mays.

Opposite: Fans soon began to expect catches like this one by the great Willie Mays.

Just when I was ready to concede that perhaps all the great days were of the past, Willie Mays made a play that will probably be talked of as long as fans sit around winter stoves and hash over the great feats of the game. Willie is a Negro boy of nineteen, who broke in with the Giants last year after the season had started and, in Leo's opinion, is the greatest prospect baseball has turned up in years. In an interview with Frank Graham, of the *New York Journal-American*, Leo stated flatly that he wouldn't trade Willie, even up, for Stan Musial or Ted Williams, or any other player in baseball.

"He may end up as the greatest player baseball has ever seen," said Leo. "I think that's how he *will* end up."

The Giants had a 2–1 lead over the Dodgers in the eighth inning of a bitterly contested game at the Polo Grounds. The Dodgers were at bat with one man out, Billy Cox on third, Don Newcombe first, and Carl Furillo at the plate. Furillo hit a fly ball to right center, which Mays captured after a long run. Since he was headed toward right field when he caught the ball, and was being propelled still further in the wrong direction by the impetus of his dash, Willie was in no position for a throw. Cox was tagged up at third, ready for the dash to the plate. Nobody in the ball park had the faintest idea that a throw would do any good. But we were about to witness a remarkable thing! As he caught the ball, Willie stopped dead, pivoted about to his left like a second baseman completing a double play—and fired the ball on a dead line toward the infield. Wes Westrum took it on one hop at the plate—and Cox was out by five feet!

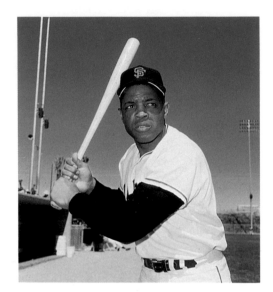

"That's the finest play I've ever seen," cried Eddie Brannick, "and I've been watching baseball for forty years!"

All I know is that I have never seen a crowd so electrified. After the first stunned moment of silence, a roar went up that was enough to blow the roof of the Polo Grounds over into the Harlem River. Willie explained later that as he ran for the ball he figured out what he would do—the quick stop, the pivot, and then a throw aimed at the letters on the shirt of Whitey Lockman, our first baseman, who, on cut-off plays, stands in the middle of the infield on a line between the outfielder and the catcher.

"What would you have done if I had cut off that ball?" Whitey teased Leo later in the clubhouse. The cut-off is used in this way to keep the man on first from advancing.

"You'd have found your brains all over the pitcher's mound," said Leo grimly.

"I'm not sure I know just what the hell charisma is, but I get the feeling it's Willie Mays," said Cincinnati star Ted Kluszewski.

1954: THE MOST SHOCKING WORLD SERIES OF THE FIFTIES

The Cleveland Indians, led by slugging Larry Doby and Al Rosen and twenty-three-game-winners Bob Lemon and Early Wynn, had posted an astounding record of 111–43. The New York Giants, experts agreed, had little chance in the Series against the Cleveland juggernaut. But, as Roger Kahn reported in "1 . . . 2 . . . 3 . . . 4 . . . & Bingo," in the October 11, 1954, *Sports Illustrated,* experts can be wrong.

Only once during the New York Giants' annihilation of the Cleveland Indians did Al Lopez, the Cleveland manager, permit himself the luxury of rage.

For four days Lopez suffered in reflected humiliation while the Giants swept the 1954 World Series from the Indians, four games to none. The sweep was an achievement baseball men had insisted was impossible. Bookmakers admitted it was possible, but rated the possibility at 22-to-1. Yet as the incredible victimized him, Al Lopez remained soft-spoken save for a single interlude after the second game when Early Wynn failed, when the Indian attack failed for the second time and when ultimate defeat became a clear and present danger.

Reporters were admitted to the visitors' clubhouse at the Polo Grounds five minutes after the second game ended. They gathered in a tight circle about Lopez. There were some good questions and some bad. At first Lopez answered in whispers.

"What was the turning point today?" one reporter asked.

"There wasn't any turning point," Lopez murmured.

"There's got to be a turning point," the reporter insisted. "What was it?"

For some journeyman players, the World Series provides an unexpected chance to shine. A case in point is Dusty Rhodes (here, arriving at home after his game-winning Game One home run). He hit two home runs and drove in seven runs to lead the Giants to their stunning sweep of the Cleveland Indians in the 1954 World Series.

"There wasn't any, I'm telling you," Lopez repeated, breaking out of a whisper.

"Was the turning point when Doby couldn't catch that ball Rhodes hit?" the reporter persisted thickly.

"Now goddam," Lopez shouted. "What are you trying to do. Ask your questions and answer them, too? Goddam. What are you trying to do?"

When the series ended Saturday some reporters tried to plant in Lopez' mouth more words about a turning point. With considerable difficulty synthetic quotes were created. Actually, as Lopez knew, the 1954 World Series was without one single hinge. There was a great many points at which things turned against the Indians. To equate one against the other is to equate the destructiveness of a teaspoonful against a tablespoon of uranium.

The first game, which the Giants won 5-to-2, was a turning point because it had been generally assumed that Bob Lemon, Cleveland's starting pitcher, was stronger and better than the Giants' Sal Maglie.

The second game, which the Giants won 3-to-1, was a turning point because it had been generally assumed that Early Wynn, pitcher of three two-hit games in September, was unbeatable in a clutch.

The third game, which the Giants won 6-to-2, was a turning point because it had been generally assumed that the Indians were waiting to sandbag the Giants at Cleveland's Municipal Stadium.

The fourth game, which the Giants won 7-to-4, was a turning point because it had been generally assumed that the Indians would win the World Series.

In the first inning of the first game the Indians looked good. They scored two runs when Vic Wertz made the first of his eight hits, a triple to right center field that batted in Al Smith and Bobby Avila. Then the Indians, winners of more games than any American League team in history, went into a miniature decline and fall. The Giants tied the score in the third inning. In the sixth, with Wertz at third base, Jim Hegan bounced fiercely to Henry Thompson at third. Thompson fought the grounder with both hands until it surrendered. His throw to first base was in time by half a step.

"When that ball squirted away," Thompson said, "all I was thinking was I gotta get that son of a buck over to first base."

In the eighth inning, with two Indians on base and no one out, Vic Wertz hit a ball 450 feet, where Willie Mays caught it. Never before had so unbelievable a catch been seen and disbelieved by so many.

"Was it real?" someone asked Al Dark, the Giants' captain, later.

"It was real," Dark said, as though he had only then convinced himself.

But there was at least one more turning point in that first game. With two Giants on base in the tenth inning, a high-living Southerner named Jim Rhodes pinch-hit for Monte Irvin and lifted a fly into the breeze that blew toward right field. Bobby Avila, Cleveland's second baseman, started back for the ball. A customer in the right-field stands muffed it. Three runs scored; the Giants had won.

Next afternoon at the Polo Grounds the crowd sagged below 50,000 and there were proportionately fewer turning points. Johnny Antonelli, the Giants' young left-hander, made his first pitch a fast ball and Al Smith, Cleveland's young left fielder, hit the fast ball to the roof of the upper deck. Thereafter 13 Indians reached base and though none was observed biting dust, none scored, either.

Early Wynn pitched four perfect innings, then two Giants reached base and Rhodes again hit for Irvin. This time he pinch-popped a single to short center field beyond the reach of Larry Doby. The Indians were impaled on a sharp new turning point.

"He's a pretty fair hitter," said Giant Scout Tom Sheehan of Rhodes.

"He's a County Fair hitter. He goes up there and swings."

Then the series moved to Cleveland, where one store was caught with a sign showing. "Congratulations, Indians," the sign in the window read. "You're sitting on top of the world."

Lemon and Wynn had been beaten. Al Rosen, Cleveland's clean-up hitter, was crippled by a pulled leg muscle. Rosen sat down as Mike Garcia got up to pitch the third game. A 37-year-old veteran named Hank Majeski took over third base from Rosen. All season subs had come through for Cleveland, but by this time a great many points had turned. Majeski went hitless, Rhodes pinch-hit a two-run single, Ruben Gomez outpitched Garcia and the Indians were down three games.

"No sense waiting for the spring," Rosen said a day later as he prepared to go back to third base. "Lemon goes fine with two days' rest," said Al Lopez when someone wondered what had become of Bobby Feller.

A small left-hander named Don Liddle held the Indians while Lemon did not go fine and the Giants moved ahead, 7-to-0. Cleveland fought back too late when Majeski pinch-hit a three-run homer and when a rally knocked out Liddle for Hoyt Wilhelm in the seventh. Wilhelm stopped it, but another rally knocked him out for Antonelli with one out in the eighth. Johnny whipped a curve past Wertz's bat for a second out. With two strikes on Wally Westlake, Antonelli tossed a change-up pitch and Westlake watched it drift over the plate. When he did so, Cleveland's hotelkeepers who had raised prices for rooms, barkeeps who had raised prices for drinks and Cleveland's fans who had wanted to see another game on Sunday, knew what the Indians knew, too. The Giants were in.

"A big dead salami," the Giants' Joe Garagiola shouted during the clubhouse celebration. "Johnny threw Westlake a big dead salami."

"The boys did it all," Manager Leo Durocher shouted.

"Leo," said a moist-eyed reporter. "You managed great."

"The boys did it all," Durocher said in normal tones.

"World Champions," Whitey Lockman, the first baseman, said quietly. "What do you know. But I bet they'd like another crack at us."

Big Jim Rhodes spoke for the majority. Big Jim stuck a cigar in his mouth. "Hey!" he shouted. "Where's the champagne?"

Afterward there came perspective and with perspective came questions. Were the Indians' 111 victories merely the reflection of a fairly good team in a terribly weak American League? Had Rosen's leg been sound and Larry Doby's shoulder uninjured, would there have been a struggle? Or were the Giants baseball's supreme opportunists, unbeatable always in 1954 because of a Mays catch, a Thompson stop or a Rhodes pinch-hit home run? The answers, if they exist at all, are as elusive as the single turning point the reporter tried to get from Al Lopez.

But one Giant official had all the answers he needed. "We didn't just beat Cleveland," he insisted. "We showed those Yankees up but good."

MICKEY MANTLE AND ROGER MARIS: M FOR MURDER

The Mick, of course, was the Yankees' greatest star during the fifties and early sixties, ending his career with 536 home runs (eighth most of all time), 1710 RBI, and 153 stolen bases—a total that would have been far higher if bad knees

hadn't prematurely robbed him of his speed. Roger Maris, the man who hit sixty-one home runs in 1961, breaking Babe Ruth's thirty-four-year-old record, was only briefly in Mantle's class as a power hitter. As Jim Murray wrote in "M for Murder" (originally published in the *Los Angeles Times*, reprinted in *The Best of Jim Murray*, 1965), for one season, though, the Yankees boasted the two most feared sluggers in the game.

The young Mickey Mantle, before leg injuries condemned him to constant pain, seems to enjoy an earth-scattering practice slide.

The Mick: Older and heavier, but still possessing that deadly swing.

When he was only one day old, Mickey Charles Mantle had a baseball put in his hand by his father. When he was four years old, he had a bat put in his hand. When he was five years old, he began to have curve balls thrown at him.

Mickey Mantle has been a ballplayer all his life. Oddly enough, it has never been clearly established he wanted to be. The pay is good, the hours can't be beat, but the central fact is Mickey had no freer choice than a kid who's led down a coal mine in his first pair of long pants.

Mickey's father had the best of intentions. It was precisely to escape the zinc mines of Commerce, Oklahoma, where he spent his own life, that he thrust baseball on his son.

In 1946, Mickey had to plead to be allowed to try football. His father relented. The result was a shin bruise in a pileup which was to affect his entire life. When it swelled alarmingly, a specialist was consulted. "You have osteomyelitis," he told Mickey.

The strange story of Mickey Mantle's career after that shattering incident is told in a revealing biography by Dick Schaap, *Mickey Mantle, the Indispensable Yankee,* an indispensable book.

No one brought more inborn talent to the big leagues than Mickey Mantle. He was a switch hitter because his father made him. He was a hitter because nature made him. Yet there were times when he wept with frustration and wanted to quit. His father, of course, wouldn't let him.

When Mickey appeared in the Yankee training camp in Arizona in 1951, the sportswriters pulled out all the stops. Ty Cobb had been born again. The journalist, Tom Meany, surveyed this chorus of praise in some amazement and then suggested perhaps Mantle skip playing altogether and "go straight to Cooperstown and get in a glass cage."

There were some doctors who thought it might be a fine idea. Osteomyelitis, it happens, is an infection of the bone marrow which can be controlled but rarely cured. A membrane like the inner covering of an egg covers up the infection giving the appearance of healing. But any jar or bruise breaks it open again. Baseball is not the happiest environment for a man carrying its bacteria around with him.

For an ordinary mortal, Mantle's ten-year achievements in baseball—.307 lifetime average, 993 runs batted in, 323 home runs, 1611 base hits—are perfectly astonishing. For a man with osteomyelitis, they are incredible.

Yet, it is a melancholy fact that Yankee fans ring each other up on game day at the Stadium with a bright idea: "Let's go out and boo Mantle." He has been upbraided by his own manager, riddled by the press, and even a rival manager, Al Lopez, who should have been glad of it, was moved once to mourn "Mickey Mantle is the most talented natural ballplayer I've ever seen but he hasn't fully capitalized on his gifts."

Part of the trouble is Mantle keeps coming up with mysterious leg injuries which are always explained away in terms of the familiar sprains, tears, and Charley horses all baseball is prey to. Forgotten is the fact that some doctors, on the first outbreak of Mickey's bone disease, counseled amputation as a hedge against a painful late life—or even an absence of one.

Mickey has seldom said anything—not even when he takes the field with a limp and the inflammatory words "dogging it" get thrown around loosely.

He has continued to play superior baseball—and kept his problems to himself. When I discussed his disease with him, Mickey only said "It's arrested now. I don't think about it."

Once, when a group of Dodgers were heaping some coal on the legend of Mantle's apparent indifference, Jackie Robinson broke up the discussion by noting quietly, "Look, we got plenty of guys worse than he is. Trouble is, we ain't got anybody as good."

Mickey's burden with the Yankees was that he was replacing Joe DiMaggio—virtually alone. The Yankees had always had its assassins in tandem—Ruth and Gehrig, Gehrig and DiMaggio, DiMaggio and Keller. DiMag quit when Mickey was a pup.

Mickey now has an accomplice. Roger Maris. It puts the pressure on a pitcher. Both benefit. And the press box is alive with alliteration. Mantle and Maris have become "Dial M for Murder," "Murder and Mayhem," "Maul and Mangle," and, in

*"Murder and Mayhem" with
former president Harry S Truman.*

For Mantle, much of a brilliant career was a day-to-day struggle.

Opposite: No one ever patrolled right field like the electrifying Roberto Clemente.

the words of Eli Grba, who has to get them out, "Thunder and Lightning." Around the league, the managers term them "Messrs. Assault and Battery."

In 1927, Ruth and Gehrig broke the record for home runs by teammates when Babe hit 60 and Gehrig 47. I asked Mickey in the dressing room what the chances were for the M-Squad.

Mickey grinned. "Yeah, I read about that." He turned to Maris. "We should do it, Rog—if you get 70." "I was counting on you," countered Maris.

Funny thing is, they both could be right.

SNAPSHOTS OF CLEMENTE

If Willie Mays allowed his joy to carry him, Roberto Clemente seemed driven by darker emotions. Throughout his short life (he died in a plane crash on New Year's Eve, 1972, while ferrying supplies to victims of a Nicaraguan earthquake), the great Latin star seemed to keep much of himself hidden from all but his closest friends. But like Mays, Clemente garnered Hall of Fame credentials as a hitter—.317 lifetime average, 3000 hits—while stunning observers with his incomparable skills as a rightfielder. In *Playing the Field* (1987), Jim Kaplan recounts some of Clemente's most awe-inspiring feats.

On the field, Clemente was stern and unsmiling—all business.

There was another landslide election in 1984. Responding to an informal poll, scouts, managers, coaches, former teammates, and opponents overwhelmingly selected the late Pirate Roberto Clemente as the greatest defensive rightfielder they'd seen.

They remember him in a series of surrealistic stills:

Clemente, spiderlike, back to the plate, climbing the Astrodome fence. His body is outlined against the yellow home run stripe eight feet off the ground. The date is June 15, 1971. Clemente has just made a game-saving, one-handed catch of Bob Watson's line drive. A moment later Clemente will crash into the fence and suffer a bruised left ankle, a swollen left elbow, and a bloodied left knee. And hang onto the ball. "Best catch I've ever seen," Astro manager Harry Walker said at the time. Bill Mazeroski, a Pirate second baseman from 1956 to 1972, wasn't so sure. "This was a lot like the one Roberto made off Willie Mays in 1961," he said.

Clemente, suspended horizontally three feet off the ground, his body at right angles to home plate. He has just made the kind of play he's best remembered for—fielding a hit at the line, spinning around, and leaving his feet while throwing to second or third. Clemente could also play caroms off the fence and hold runners to singles. He once caught a fly 420 feet from home and threw out a runner who had tagged at third. "I saw someone hit a fly to short right," says longtime Cincinnati first baseman Tony Perez. "Lee May was leaning on the third-base bag. Clemente got the ball on a bounce and threw out Lee by three or four feet at home."

Clemente fielding a bunt! With runners on first and second and the Pirate shortstop covering third, Houston's Bob Lillis bunted through the shortstop hole. Clemente raced over from right, fielded the ball in short left-center, and threw out base-runner Walt Bond, who was attempting to go from first to third.

Clemente sitting up or lying face-down. He has just made one of his innumerable sliding catches.

Clemente, reeling, like a man who has just been shot. A ball he has lost in the lights has just hit him in the chest. He will recover to catch the ball before it hits the ground.

Clemente himself is not pictured in the final still. There's just a ball flying over the right-field stands in Forbes Field. "Orlando Cepeda of the Giants hit a line drive down the runway and past the bullpen, which was behind the stands and out of sight," recalls Phil Dorsey, a Clemente confidant. "Roberto picked up the ball and threw out the baserunner, Mays, at the plate. Damndest play I ever saw on a ball field." But not a unique one for Clemente. On other occasions he went into the bullpen to make blind throws and catch Cincinnati and Houston runners at third.

As a high school player Clemente switched from shortstop to the outfield. When he was 18, the Dodgers were conducting a tryout for 72 youngsters at Sixto Escobar Stadium in San Juan, Puerto Rico. "The first thing I did at the workout was ask kids to throw from the outfield," Dodger executive vice president Al Campanis recalled years later. "This kid Clemente throws a bullet from center, on the fly. I couldn't believe it. '*Uno Mas!*' I shout, and he does it again. Then we have them run 60 yards. The first time I clock him he does it in 6.4 seconds—in full uniform. '*Uno Mas!*' I shout, and he does it again."

The Dodgers eventually signed Clemente for a $10,000 bonus, left him unprotected on their Montreal farm club, and lost him to the Pirates, who drafted him on November 22, 1954. As a big-league rightfielder in 1955–72, Clemente won 12 Gold Gloves and a league outfield mark of five assist titles. Players referred to his arm as El Bazooka. Its accuracy he attributed to throwing the javelin in high school, its strength to his mother. "She could throw a ball from second to home with something on it," he once said. "I got my arm from her."

"I remember Roberto coming out early to work on his throwing," says Phil Dorsey. "He'd set metal baskets on their sides at second and third. A coach, Ron Northey, would hit balls off the screen and Roberto would work for hours retrieving them and throwing them into the baskets."

"Clemente was to right field what Ozzie Smith is to shortstop," says Lillis. A fitting slogan for a landslide winner.

Brooks Robinson at third base: No line drive or wicked grounder was safe from his vacuum glove.

DISCOVERING A STAR: BROOKS ROBINSON

In this letter, an unsolicited report to the Baltimore Orioles by ex–major-leaguer Lindsay Deal on a seventeen-year-old high-schooler destined for the Hall of Fame (and for recognition as perhaps the best defensive third baseman ever), catch a glimpse of the high-risk and unscientific world of scouting.

February 13, 1955

I am writing you in regard to a kid named Brooks Robinson. I think he measures up to having a good chance in major league baseball. I think he is a natural third baseman although he has been playing both second and third. He will be 18 years old on May 18 and graduates from Little Rock Senior High School on May 27. He is 6 ft. 1 in. and weighs 175. His physique is outstanding for a boy this age. He bats right and throws right. He is no speed demon but neither is he a truck horse. I believe in a year or two he will be above the average in speed. He hit well over .400 last year in

Brooks Robinson: Smooth, fluid, totally self-confident.

American Legion baseball, including all tournament games. At the tournament in Altus, Oklahoma, he was awarded the trophy for being the outstanding player. Brooks has a lot of power, baseball savvy and is always cool when the chips are down. This boy is the best prospect I've seen since Billy Goodman came to Atlanta to play when I was playing there. That's the reason I'm contacting you. I thought you might be interested in him and able to make as good an offer as anyone else. Otherwise, I wouldn't have bothered you with it.

This boy can go to most any University in the Southwest on a scholarship and will do so if he doesn't receive a fair bonus and contract in major league baseball. I know his parents well; in fact, we attend the same church. I have talked the situation over with them to some extent. Although no figures were quoted, I don't believe they will be unreasonable. However, the team with the best offer will get him, come May 27. If you are interested, I think you could work to an advantage through me.

He has been bird-dogged by scouts for the past three years. Here are some of the clubs that I know are definitely interested: Patterson of the Phillies, Camp and McHale of Detroit, Donald of the Yankees, Jonnard of the Giants now with Kansas City, Rice of the Red Sox, Hahan of the Cardinals and a scout from the White Sox. . . .

Sincerely,

Lindsay Deal

JUAN MARICHAL: FIFTY CENTS FOR THE SHOEMAKER

Juan Marichal (243 career wins, six twenty-win seasons), one of the first of a flood of talented ballplayers from the Dominican Republic, tells of modest baseball beginnings in *A Pitcher's Story* (1967), by Juan Marichal with Charles Einstein.

Marichal's scythelike windup is perhaps the most recognizable pitching motion of all time.

For baseball equipment when you were a farm boy in the Dominican Republic, there seldom was money, but you seldom needed it. All you needed was fifty cents, to pay the shoemaker, and you were in business.

You made your bats, cutting them from the branches of the *vasima* tree, which is like an apple tree, only bigger. Then you would let them dry in the sun, and the wood would become lighter when the sun got to it. You would then trim the bat and rub it so the handle part was smooth. Now you had a bat.

Gloves were no problem. You took a piece of burlap, framed it around a sheet of cardboard, sewed up the sides with fishing line, and bent the whole thing in the middle. Now everybody's glove looked like a first baseman's mitt. But you had a glove, and the glove even had padding—the cardboard.

Then you would go to the golf links at Monte Cristi and find an old golf ball and take the inside—the center—from this golf ball, then take a woman's stocking, unravel it, and wind it patiently around the center until it was the right size. Then you took your fifty cents and went to a shoemaker and gave it to him to sew a leather cover onto the ball.

So that was what the shoemaker and the fifty cents were for, but if you did not have fifty cents you could get almost the same effect by wrapping the ball with friction tape instead.

1966: THE METS LUCK OUT

From the April 4 *Daily News,* a small item about the man who would in three years lead the perennially woeful New York Mets to the 1969 World Championship: George Thomas "Tom" Seaver, three-time winner of the Cy Young Award.

The Mets received permission from Baseball Commissioner William D. Eckert today to sign controversial college pitcher George Seaver to a $40,000 bonus contract.

Seaver, 21, had his college eligibility cut short when he prematurely signed an agreement with Atlanta's Richmond farm club.

Seaver was selected by Atlanta in last January's high school and college draft and signed to a $40,000 contract by Richmond in February.

Eckert, however, disapproved the pact because the University of Southern California had begun its intercollegiate season and the signing of Seaver was ruled a violation of the college code. Eckert fined Richmond $500 and declared the team ineligible to sign the youngster for the next three years.

USC subsequently voided Seaver's eligibility, despite the fact he had never received any payment from a professional baseball club.

Other clubs were permitted to bid for Seaver's services, but Eckert said that a team signing the pitcher must agree to the $40,000 price since the youngster originally had signed in good faith for that figure.

The Mets, Indians and Phillies expressed a willingness to the terms and agreed to draw for Seaver. The Mets won.

1968: AL KALINE'S GREATEST MOMENT

In a twenty-two-year career with the Detroit Tigers, Al Kaline amassed 3007 hits, 1583 RBI, and a batting average of .297. He reached the World Series just once, however, when he was thirty-three years old and his skills had already begun to erode. But as Jerry Green's October 11, 1968, *Detroit News* report on the seventh game of the great Tigers-Cardinal series shows, Kaline's chance for glory did not come too late.

Opposite: Tom Seaver came to win, and he brought the rest of the hitherto dismal Mets with him.

Al Kaline had been waiting for this for 16 years, ever since he was a teenage big leaguer.

Now it was the moment, the Tigers had been World Champions for 10 precious minutes.

"It was worth waiting 16 years," said Kaline, now 33 and often hurt and without many seasons left.

"I'd seen my other World Series in the country club, watching on TV. I considered people lucky to be in the Series. I felt that way when Minnesota got in three years ago with a couple of kids their first year up.

A quiet superstar, Detroit's Al Kaline finally got the chance to shine in the 1968 World Series—and led the Tigers to a thrilling seven-game victory over the St. Louis Cardinals.

Opposite: "The greatest pitcher I ever faced," Al Kaline said of the Cardinals' Bob Gibson.

"I knew all along I'd get in a Series someday, maybe as a pinch hitter, hopefully with Detroit."

Pinch hitter, indeed. Al Kaline, hurt twice and a platoon player this pennant winning World Championship year for the Tigers, was the hitting star of the World Series. A spot had been opened for him in a daring maneuver and he made his manager a sage.

Kaline zoomed through his first World Series with a .379 batting average on 11 hits in 29 trips. He hit two doubles, two homers and drove in eight runs.

"I never expected to have this good a Series," said Kaline. "I was one of the lucky ones."

He was standing away from the tumult yesterday afternoon when it ended in victory, typical in a season of comebacks. He did not participate in the champagne squirting which occupied the celebration of the younger World Champions.

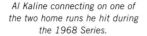

Al Kaline connecting on one of the two home runs he hit during the 1968 Series.

Kaline held his own bottle of champagne around the neck and occasionally sipped from it, sometimes sharing it with others.

He talked quietly, without exuberance. In his happiest hour, Kaline behaved exactly in the manner he has played through his 16 frustrating years.

"Bob Gibson is the greatest pitcher I ever faced," said Kaline. "To beat him and win the World Series all in one game is really great.

"We just wanted to get into the seventh game real bad—for our pride after the way we played the first two games in Detroit.

"Our team made a great comeback. We were embarrassed the way we played. We just didn't want to get beat four games to one. If we got beat, we wanted to get beat by Gibson because he's the best.

"We bounced back all year like this. We just got a bunch of hits together in this game, just like we've been doing all year, in the seventh, eighth and ninth innings.

"The big secret to this club in the late innings is everybody just goes for base hits, they stop trying for the long ball."

So it was as the Tigers dramatically won the World Series over the Cardinals. It happened that way in the decisive game yesterday. It happened that way Monday when the Tigers, behind 3–1 in the Series, rallied and won on Kaline's single in the seventh inning.

Al Kaline had scored the winning run the night the Tigers won the pennant, a contribution he had predicted he would make. But such contributions were fewer than usual this pennant year.

Often he was on the bench, platooned or playing in foreign positions such as first base or left field.

Manager Mayo Smith's bold decision to switch Mickey Stanley to shortstop was caused by a need for Kaline in right field in the Series. It happened after Kaline talked to Smith and told him he would not be upset if he did not play in the World Series.

Kaline has said he does not regard himself as one of baseball's superstars. But he probably reached the height of his career in the World Series. It had to outshine the batting championship he won at age 20 in 1955 because in the Series he was playing in a national spotlight.

His World Series was superior to anything Ty Cobb did the three years his Tigers won the pennant in 1907–08–09.

"I had a great Series," Kaline said sincerely. "This is the way I play. In a big series I tend to do the right thing at the right time."

Stan Musial, the greatest of all the Cardinals and now senior vice-president of the club, walked in to congratulate Kaline. The two had similarities on the playing field— quiet and competent.

"I hope we're in it together next year, Al," said Musial.

"We'll be in it," said Kaline.

HANK AARON: FOR JACKIE

Everyone always thought that Babe Ruth's record of 714 lifetime home runs was unreachable. In *I Had a Hammer* (1991), by Henry Aaron with Lonnie Wheeler, Aaron talks about one of the people who helped him achieve a new record: 755.

I hit thirty-four homers in 1972, which left me only forty-one shy of Ruth. It seemed unlikely that I would hit forty-one or forty-two homers in 1973, at the age of thirty-nine, but I was only one year removed from hitting forty-seven, and I was powerfully motivated on several fronts. The most basic motivation was the pure ambition to break such an important and long-standing barrier. Along with that would come the recognition that I thought was long overdue me: I would be out of the shadows. I can't deny that I was also very interested in the financial benefits that the record would surely bring. Then there was the sense of doing something for my race. I felt stronger and stronger about that as the years went on—as I read about people like Martin Luther King and listened to people like Jesse Jackson, and as I saw what went on around me in baseball, and in Atlanta. The hate mail drove me, too. In 1972, when people finally realized that I was climbing up Ruth's back, the "Dear Nigger" letters started showing up with alarming regularity. They told me that no nigger had any right to go where I

Above: Hank Aaron's record-setting swing.

"It was like I was running in a bubble," Hank Aaron said of his triumphant trip around the bases following his epochal blast.

was going. There's no way to measure the effect that those letters had on me, but I like to think that every one of them added another home run to my total.

There was one last thing that hardened my resolve after the 1972 season. Late in October, Jackie Robinson died. It was just a couple of weeks after he had been in Cincinnati for the World Series. His hair was white, he walked with a cane, and he was going blind with diabetes, but he was still a spellbinding presence. Jackie gave a talk while he was in Cincinnati and said that until the time came when there was a black man calling the shots from the dugout or from a swivel chair in the front office, baseball would have its head buried in the sand. I wasn't there, but I understand that after his talk, Jackie wandered into the Oakland clubhouse, thinking that some of the black players might want to come up and talk to him, maybe even say thank you. But none of them did, and after a while, Jackie just walked out with his cane and went back to his hotel room. It was the last time he was seen in public.

A lot of the black players from the early days were at his funeral, but I was shocked at how few of the active players showed up. It made me more determined than ever to keep Jackie's dream alive, and the best way I could do that was to become the all-time home run champion in the history of the game that had kept out black people for more than sixty years. I owed it to Jackie. I just wish he could have seen me do it. God, he would have been proud.

1975: RED SOX VS. REDS, GAME SIX

An inside view of what many people consider to be the greatest World Series game ever played. From *Joe Morgan: A Life in Baseball,* by Joe Morgan and David Falkner (1993).

The Red Sox jumped off to a first-inning 3–0 lead on a homer by Fred Lynn and then went into cruise control with Tiant doing his thing. But, once again, he did not have his best stuff. The ball was coming up to the plate the way it did in the fourth game rather than the first. We rallied to tie the game in the fifth, went ahead by two runs in the seventh, added another in the eighth; it looked almost certain that we were going to be the world champions.

When Bernie Carbo came up in the bottom of the eighth with two men on and two out, I still thought we were going to make it. Rawly Eastwick had come into the game two batters earlier and had gotten them. He was pitching outstanding relief for us—and he clearly was in control in the situation. Eastwick got two strikes on Carbo, and made him look bad in doing it. Then he threw him a pitch that, from where I stood, looked unhittable. It was a sharp-breaking slider, down and in, and Carbo swung at it awkwardly. It was a funny swing, the kind a batter makes when he is completely fooled. Carbo barely touched the ball—it was just a tick—but he fouled it off. When Eastwick came back with a fastball, Carbo hit it into the center-field bleachers—and we were tied.

*Boston's Carl Yastrzemski:
So close, yet . . .*

I remember everything then went blank for me. I knew the second the ball was hit that it was out. I don't think I heard the crowd or even saw Carbo circling the bases. I came to thinking only that we were tied, that the rug had been pulled out from under us just at the point where we were going to be world champs. I thought of that Oakland Series in '72 and that maybe we were snakebit.

The game continued, more like a war of attrition than a baseball game. Somewhere in here we tied a World Series record when an eighth pitcher from our team entered the game. There were maybe twelve pitchers in all for both teams, also a record or near-record. It figured to happen with Captain Hook, Sparky Anderson, managing one team. In any case, it became clear to players on either team, to the fans, to everyone watching, that this game could only end on some kind of dramatic, spectacular note.

In the eleventh inning, we got a man on and with one out I had a chance to hit. I got the pitch I wanted from the Red Sox reliever, Dick Drago, and I hit the ball hard to right. I got a little bit on top of it, I had too much top hand in my swing, but the ball was going to carry out of the park anyway. But because of the topspin on the ball, I kept watching Dwight Evans: and he didn't seem to be giving up. I said to myself, Whoa, where does he think he's going, he can't get to that. But he kept going back, back, and then he leaped—and caught the ball. I couldn't believe it: and, neither, apparently, did anyone else watching the game. It was one of the great catches ever—and what was more, because Evans was a supremely intelligent player, he remained in the game all the while. As soon as he made the catch, he wheeled away from the grandstand, remembering that was only the second out in the inning, and threw to first base—knowing that the runner, like everyone else, had thought the ball was out. This great catch was now turned into an even more impressive inning-ending double play.

There was even a spooky side to this play. Sometime later, I learned that Evans, just before I hit that ball, had a picture pop into his head where he saw himself going into the stands to take a home run away from me! That's hard for me to believe, but in this particular game, anything was possible.

When Fisk hit his game-winning homer in the bottom of the twelfth, my reaction, standing at second base, was a bit strange. The first thing I did was to wait to see if the ball was going to be fair or foul—like Fisk, like everyone else. The angle I had made it especially hard to tell.

But then, when I saw that the ball was fair, I had no sense of disappointment or dejection. I still had a job to do. With the crowd screaming and the Red Sox players leaping from the dugout, I stayed in place waiting to make sure that Fisk actually touched the bases as he made his way around the diamond. Imagine what would have happened if he had missed one.

Joe Morgan about to put the Reds ahead to stay with the ninth-inning, no-out Game Seven single that decided the classic '75 Series.

Our clubhouse was like a morgue. But there were some guys, especially Pete [Rose], talking about what an honor it was to play in such a game. That's not what I felt, though.

*"I always felt we were the best,"
said Joe Morgan after the Reds'
victory. "Now I can say it and no
one can say anything different."*

When the writers came to me wanting to know how I felt, I said, "Hey, it was a good game." They wanted more. They wanted to know what the effect of losing a game we had just about won would have on us in the seventh game the next day. I said what I honestly felt, that it would have no effect whatsoever. "When you come out here tomorrow," I said, "you'll see the best team in baseball go at 'em again. And we will win. Hey, I'll take these guys every day of the week in the seventh game of the World Series."

Morgan's optimism was warranted. The Reds came back from a three-run deficit to defeat the Red Sox 4–3, getting a run in the ninth on a two-out single by—you guessed it—Joe Morgan. Everyone agreed that Game Seven would have been one of the most memorable games of any World Series—if it hadn't come directly after Game Six.

THE SHAPE OF THINGS TO COME: FREE AGENCY

A report by Sports Editor Bob Maisel in *The Morning Sun* (Baltimore), November 14, 1975.

It hasn't received much publicity, but starting this week, some of the most important decisions in the history of baseball are scheduled to be made. Specifically, they involve a testing of the reserve clause by [pitchers] Dave McNally and Andy Messersmith.

So little has been said about the whole thing that I had forgotten about it, until a phone conversation with [Orioles executive] Frank Cashen yesterday. I had been trying to talk with Cashen about something else, but he had been out of town for several days.

"I was in New York," he said. "I'm on the player relations committee, and we've had some things to talk about, including the arbitration meetings coming up on the McNally-Messersmith thing. This is about as important as anything we've faced in a long time. If we get an adverse ruling this time, we're really in trouble."

That brought it all back into focus. Messersmith didn't sign his contract last year, because he couldn't get together with the Dodgers. McNally had similar difficulties with Montreal and never got around to signing. He subsequently left the ball club with the intention of retiring from the game, but Messersmith stayed active.

Baseball contracts contain a clause which gives the club the right to a one year renewal in case the player doesn't sign. In this challenge against the reserve clause, it is being contended that both McNally and Messersmith have now fulfilled that one year obligation, and have earned the right to be declared free agents.

Baseball, on the other hand, contends the renewal clause is a perpetual thing, which renews itself every year, thus binding a player to one organization until it makes some disposition of him. The cases are scheduled to be heard, next Friday and the following Monday, before arbitrator Peter Seitz. Yes, that's the same gentleman who made the decision granting Catfish Hunter his free agency, setting off the bidding contest eventually won by the Yankees for about $3.7 million.

If Seitz makes the same ruling on McNally and Messersmith, you've got the beginning of chaos in baseball, with more and more players playing out their options and auctioning themselves off.

They can do that in football now, but the Rozelle rule dictates that the team losing a player must be given equal payment in return. If the two clubs can't get together on the payment, then commissioner Pete Rozelle arbitrarily makes the decision for them, and there is no appeal. That is the rule being tested in court by the Players Association now. Baseball has no such rule, because it has never been called upon to defend the renewal clause . . . until now.

The facts in the Messersmith-McNally cases are not the same as those involved in the Hunter case. Charley Finley was ruled to have failed to fulfill the terms of Hunter's contract, thus nullifying the contract and making Hunter a free agent.

The contracts of McNally and Messersmith were not breached. They simply were never signed, so arbitrator Seitz will be faced with an entirely different set of circumstances.

The more I thought of all this, the more one thing kept bothering me. If you know Dave McNally, you also know he does not talk for effect, nor does he take obligations lightly. Why hadn't he signed a formal letter of retirement when he announced his intention of leaving the game? And, if he left Montreal to play elsewhere now, as poorly as that deal turned out for the Expos, then I'd be disappointed in him.

So, if you know a guy well, and have something on your mind, the best thing to do is ask him about it personally.

A call to his Ford dealership in Billings, Mont., got him on the phone with no trouble. There is no question he still has a soft spot for the Orioles, Baltimore, and his old team-mates.

He talked about how great it was to hear about Jim Palmer winning the Cy Young Award again, asked about Cashen going back to the brewery and being replaced by Hank Peters, also passed along best wishes to Nelson Fox, undergoing treatment at the

Cancer Research Center of University Hospital. "Nel was a great player," said Mac. "He got his 2,500th hit off me, and never let me forget it. He's one of the many milestones I've helped the hitters get over."

In answer to my questions, he replied, "I have no intention of playing baseball again. I had some great years in the game, and now I've had it. The automobile agency is going well, I have a lot to learn, am working hard at it, and really enjoy it. I'm happy right here."

Then, why the challenge to the reserve clause, and why didn't he send in his letter of retirement?

"Right after I made my decision to leave Montreal, Marvin Miller asked me not to sign the retirement papers, and he has also asked to have my name included with Messersmith's in this action," said McNally. "I gave him my okay, and that's all I know about it right now."

So, the most serious threat to the reserve clause is nearing a showdown. There could be one delay. Kansas City owner Ewing Kauffman, saying he would not have made such a substantial investment in baseball had it not been for the reserve clause, and feeling that investment is now at stake, has filed suit, contending this issue does not fall within the jurisdiction of arbitration.

A Kansas City judge must rule first next week whether the issue should go before arbitrator Seitz. If he rules against Kauffman and the other owners, then the ball is passed to Seitz.

Maybe it hasn't gotten a whole lot of buildup, but you'd better believe a lot of people in baseball will be intently following developments next week.

Pitcher Andy Messersmith,
a pivotal figure in a baseball revolution.

PART FIVE

1976–1994:
FACING THE
FUTURE

In 1972, the revitalized Players Association, headed by economist and longtime labor negotiator Marvin Miller, had flexed its muscles. In a struggle over increased pension benefits, the players walked out for thirteen days, canceling the end of spring training and eighty-six regular-season games before a settlement was reached with the owners.

That strike, however unsettling, was only a prelude to the great changes that would occur four years later, when free agency came into being. As far back as 1970, St. Louis star Curt Flood had sacrificed his career in an unsuccessful legal attempt to overturn the reserve clause on antitrust grounds. In the 1976 effort, the case was presented to arbitrator Peter Seitz, who ruled that the teams did not, in fact, have the right to keep renewing players' contracts automatically year after year. Court challenges to the decision failed, and the free agent era—with its attendant upward spiral of player salaries—had begun.

The Mets' Mookie Wilson in the 1986 World Series—just one of the thrilling postseason battles that have characterized the past decade.

Even the most casual fan knows that the years since have not been easy ones in player-owner relations. Of a litany of threatened and actual work stoppages, the most wounding were the owners' lockout of the players during spring training in 1976 and the players' midseason strike in 1981, which wiped out almost a third of the season's games. As the 1994 season approached, once again the players and owners were preparing to renegotiate their agreement.

Despite all the strife, baseball has boomed in popularity in recent years. Attendance topped fifty million for the first time in 1989 and has continued to grow, with few interruptions, since. While those against free agency predicted that it would result in a few wealthy teams dominating each league, this hasn't come to pass. As David Q. Voigt points out in an essay in the ninth edition of *The Baseball Encyclopedia* (1993), "an unprecedented spate of competitive balance made for hotly contested division races through the 1980s." Though the early nineties have seen the Pirates, Braves, and Blue Jays repeating as division winners, tight races have continued to be the rule, not the exception.

Nor has one of the other supposed ill effects of free agency—that no star player would ever spend more than a few years with the same club—come to pass. Without doubt, many players have used their freedom to move from team to team—but what tends to be forgotten is that such movement also took place before free agency. (In fact, more than seventy years ago, Fred Lieb wrote an article entitled "Few Stars Spend Entire Career with One Club" for *Baseball Magazine.*) It's true that Joe DiMaggio, Mickey Mantle, Stan Musial, and Roberto Clemente have come to represent the teams for which they played their entire careers—but so have such recent and current luminaries as Mike Schmidt, George Brett, Cal Ripken, Jr., and Kirby Puckett. And though Dave Winfield, Nolan Ryan, and Reggie Jackson have changed teams, the same can be said of Babe Ruth, Ty Cobb, Honus Wagner, and Willie Mays.

Top: "Roberto Alomar really doesn't need to get any better," said The Scouting Report: 1994 *of Toronto's star second baseman, "but he keeps doing so anyway."*

Above: Itinerant slugger Reggie Jackson hit the ball hard wherever he played.

And the game between the foul lines has never seemed healthier. Of course, older players and fans may lament the passing of some halcyon time twenty, thirty, or forty years ago. That's to be expected: The game remembered *always* seems more precious than the one in front of us. In the 1890s, retired players were unfavorably comparing the game they saw to the one they played in the sixties and seventies—and that hallowed tradition continues today.

But the truth about the 1990s brand of baseball is that after the one-dimensional play—two walks and a three-run home run—that characterized much of the fifties, and the often deadening domination by pitchers in the mid- and late sixties, fans have enjoyed a continuation of the multifaceted strategic play that began to flower in the early seventies. In any given year, one team might steal 200, or even 300, bases—as many or more than teams stole in the speed-dominated dead ball era—while another would smack 200 home runs—actually more than most teams slugged even during the height of the lively ball twenties and thirties.

This diversity of styles has led to many memorable clashes of strategic philosophies. One example: In 1985, when St. Louis played Kansas City in a scintillating seven-game World Series, the battle pitted the Cards, a team that had hit a total of 87 home runs but had stolen 314 bases, against the Royals, with 154 home runs but only 128 stolen bases. (As it turned out, each team hit only two home runs, and the Royals actually stole seven bases to the Cards' two.)

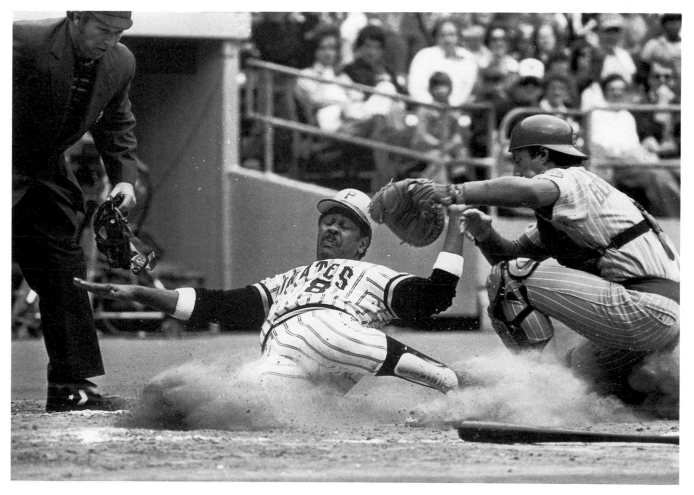

The Pirates' Willie Stargell in 1979, sliding toward a famous World Series victory and a place in the Hall of Fame.

The '85 Series was just one of the many superb late-season and postseason clashes of the past fifteen years. These include the Yankees' breathtaking one-game playoff victory over the Red Sox in '78; memorable championship series (the renowned 1986 Mets-Astros and Red Sox–Angels series and Atlanta's two seven-game nail-biters with Pittsburgh in '91 and '92); and, of course, a handful of other World Series classics.

It's easy to recapture, for instance, either in detail or scattered yet indelible images, Reggie Jackson's extraordinary '77 Series, topped by his three home runs (on three consecutive pitches) in Game Six; Pittsburgh's "We Are Family" comeback, led by Willie Stargell, from a three-games-to-one deficit to the Orioles in '79; and such turnabout Series as the Cards-Brewers in '82, Mets–Red Sox '86 (Bill Buckner's Game Six error resulting in yet another heartbreaking Boston loss, which led Roger Angell to observe that "the true function of the Red Sox may be not to win, but to provide New England authors with a theme, now that guilt and whaling have gone out of style"), and Twins-Cards '87.

Perhaps the best of all was the '91 battle between the Twins and Braves, a thrilling seven-game series that culminated in Jack Morris's ten innings of shutout ball in the Twins' 1–0 Game Seven victory. Then, just to add a 1990s slant to the concept of "America's National Game," came the back-to-back series victories by the Toronto Blue Jays in '92 and '93—the first World Series ever won by a team north of the border.

Atlanta's Dave Justice scoring at a pivotal moment in the 1991 Series against the Minnesota Twins—a seven-game thriller.

Individual achievements have also been plentiful in the modern era. Here are just a few highlights:

• In a twenty-four-year career, Steve Carlton seemed like a throwback to an earlier time: Quiet, hardworking, crafty, he amassed 329 wins, ninth most of all time, and in 1994 was elected to the Hall of Fame on the first ballot.

• Pete Rose, another kind of throwback, broke Ty Cobb's record for career hits.

• Mike Schmidt may well have been the finest power-hitting third baseman of all time, while George Brett was another marvelous offensive player at the same position.

• Ryne Sandberg, still mid-career, has already proven himself as among the top second basemen, compiling hitting and fielding statistics to rival Rogers Hornsby's and Charlie Gehringer's.

The fruits of victory: Game Six hero Joe Carter and the Toronto Blue Jays celebrate their second straight World Series championship in 1993.

Two types of superstar, 1990s style: The smooth Ryne Sandberg (left) and the explosive Rickey Henderson.

Opposite: The meeting of two future Hall of Famers: Milwaukee's leaping Robin Yount has just forced Baltimore's Cal Ripken, Jr., at second base.

Overleaf: The Yankees' gruff, hard-nosed Thurman Munson, a classic baseball personality.

• Rickey Henderson has put up numbers (including a record-breaking 130 stolen bases in 1982) that combine speed, power, and batting eye to mark him as the finest leadoff man in the history of the game.

• Has there ever been a more brilliant shortstop than Ozzie Smith? "What I set out to do was to be as entertaining as I could possibly be," Smith told author David Falkner in *Nine Sides of the Diamond* (1990)—and what could be more entertaining than baseball played on a higher plane, as the Wizard has done for more than a decade?

• Barry Bonds may not be the greatest outfielder of all time (there's plenty of competition), but his 1993 MVP award—his third—put him in heady company: Only Jimmie Foxx, Joe DiMaggio, Stan Musial, Yogi Berra, Roy Campanella, Mickey Mantle, and Mike Schmidt also won three times. Bonds, just twenty-nine years old at the start of the 1994 season, will have many opportunities to set a new record with four.

As the nineties began, a new crop of stars was emerging. Position players like Ken Griffey, Jr., Frank Thomas, Roberto Alomar, Juan Gonzalez, Mike Piazza, and Marquis Grissom, none born before 1967, show every sign of dominating All-Star lineups for the next decade, while youthful veterans like Tom Glavine, Greg Maddux, Randy Johnson, and John Wetteland should be shutting down even the most potent offenses.

Will these abundant signs of a healthy game be enough to overcome any off-the-field challenges to baseball's stability? One thing is clear when you look over the history of the game: The idea that baseball has ever been trouble-free is just another mirage cast by the untrustworthy haze of nostalgia. Ever since its modest beginnings with the Cincinnati

Giant Barry Bonds, a brilliant outfielder and clearly one of the finest offensive ballplayers of all time.

Opposite: Darryl Strawberry, one of countless players to enjoy the benefits of free agency.

Red Stockings in 1869, the game has brimmed with controversies and been threatened by events that seemed destined to destroy it altogether.

But baseball has always survived, and it will triumph over today's challenges. As late Commissioner A. Bartlett Giamatti wrote in *Take Time for Paradise* (1989), the game *must* survive, "so that the energy, the fervent zeal, the rousing excitement, and the happy camaraderie of competition we so value when we come together can continue to flourish for masses of us in the artificial but real confines of that special world, set aside but urban, the stadium holding paradise, the public place for public pleasure."

1976: A NEW WORLD DAWNS

Two Sides to Every Issue

In a December 23, 1975, decision that stunned the baseball world, arbitrator Peter Seitz declared pitchers Dave McNally and Andy Messersmith free agents, overturning the reserve clause that bound players to their teams throughout their careers. In Ralph Ray's report in the January 17, 1976, *Sporting News,* two of the men most directly affected by the decision—Commissioner Bowie Kuhn and players' counsel Dick Moss—react with arguments that demonstrate that then, as now, the two sides saw the issues from entirely different perspectives.

Baseball Commissioner Bowie Kuhn sees grave economic effects, including possible bankruptcy for some clubs, if the court upholds Seitz' action. Kuhn points out that both the San Francisco Giants and Chicago White Sox finished the 1975 season in poor financial health. The Giants at the moment are a ward of the National League, pending a deal to bring in new ownership.

The prospect of players seeking bids for their services after giving a one-year notice could push such clubs to the financial brink, Kuhn believes.

Kuhn also questions the premise that all players would benefit under a relaxed reserve system. "Top players would get a greater share of the pie," the commissioner contends, "leaving a smaller slice for average and below-average players." . . .

All that talk of financial disaster brings nary a tear to the eyes on the other side of the table. Said Dick Moss, counsel for the players' association:

"Talk of bankruptcies and grave

economic problems does not square with what management has been saying in bargaining sessions. At no time have management's representatives claimed inability to pay for proposals suggested by the players. . . .

The claim that lower ranking players would suffer under the Seitz ruling is simply an effort to create a divisive atmosphere among the players, Moss charges.

"Such a statement is rank conjecture, and it is designed to make the players feel uncomfortable," Moss said.

"As for players who move creating an imbalance, we think just the opposite would occur. It will give weaker clubs a crack at talent not now available to them," Moss suggested.

The Crux of the Matter: Does Signing Free Agents Help You Win?

The 1976 arrival of free agency to baseball was immediately proclaimed to give an unfair advantage to those teams with the money and will to invest in high-priced superstars. But in an essay in *The Bill James Player Ratings Book 1993,* James, one of the new breed of statistical analysts of the game who seek to identify the actual effects of team-building strategies rather than rely on what the conventional wisdom says, studies the issue and comes to a very different conclusion. In doing so, he provides support to those teams who believe that the way to win is to employ strong scouting and farm systems, not to patch holes with expensive outside talent.

The truth is that *all* of the teams which have adopted signing wholesale free agents as a method of a building a team have destroyed themselves. The Braves were the first big spenders. They started out with a mediocre team, and after signing Andy Messersmith, Gary Matthews, Jeff Burroughs, and a couple of other guys, they were so far out of the pennant race they couldn't even hear it rattle.

Mark Davis, one of the free agents who didn't carry his new team to greater things.

Nonetheless, other people imitated them. The Angels did the same thing. The Yankees, who entered the free agent era with an outstanding team, added a couple of free agents to that team and won the World Series —and attributed this not to the outstanding team, but to the free agents. Then they added more free agents, and more, and more, and more, until they had gutted the organization.

Well, that worked so well that the Royals decided to imitate them, and the Royals brought in Mike Boddicker and Mark Davis and Storm Davis and Wally Joyner, and then the Royals stunk. Los Angeles decided to get in the act, and the Dodgers brought in a bunch of free agents, and then they couldn't win, either.

But it never seems to sink in. Sportswriters never seem to realize that the teams they were saying were sure to win last winter because they had added the best free agents (the New York Mets and the Dodgers) didn't win. Instead, what they prefer to do is re-interpret the season so that the free agents really *were* the critical factor. See, Dave Winfield really *did* win Toronto the [1992] World Championship. Never mind that the Blue Jays were already a championship quality team, that Dave Winfield at the time was a second-line free agent who was only in the market at all because California didn't want him, and that Winfield signed with Toronto because they already had the best team in the league and he wanted to get back in the World Series.

I could understand failing to learn from the experience of the Mets, the Yankees, the Dodgers, the Royals and the Angels, if the policy of throwing money at free agents were delivering some secondary benefits. It's been ruinous. It's cost the owners millions and millions of dollars; hell, it must be a billion by now. . . .

So I simply can't understand it. I am genuinely puzzled. Somebody will sign Kirby, or Joe Carter, or David Cone, or somebody will corral two or three of the available free agents, and the sportswriters will write that they have locked up the pennant, or at least that they have improved themselves tremendously. I simply cannot understand why teams cannot learn from experience to abandon a policy which almost never works, and which is incidentally ruinous. Can you understand this? If you can, explain it to me.

MIKE SCHMIDT: "A YOUNG MAN IN A HURRY"

The dominant power hitter of the seventies and eighties, three-time MVP, and certainly the finest third baseman of his time (perhaps of any time), Mike Schmidt concluded an eighteen-year career with 548 home runs and 1595 RBI, leading the Philadelphia Phillies to five divisional championships, a pennant, and a World Series victory. But in 1973, his rookie year, he struggled so much at the bat it seemed he might go the way of countless other sluggers who couldn't hit major league pitching. In this article by Bill Conlin, published in the April 20, 1987, *Philadelphia Daily News,* Danny Ozark, Schmidt's manager that difficult year, recalls the pivotal early days of a budding Hall of Famer.

Mike Schmidt was a young man in a hurry. He knew he had come to the major leagues in less than two minor league seasons bearing a rare blend of gifts: the power to drive a baseball over any fence in any ballpark, hands quick as a featherweight boxing champion's, and above-average speed for a 6-2, 200-pounder.

Impatient? He wanted to win a home run title yesterday. Confident of his destiny? After Tom Seaver struck him out swinging in four at-bats running in Shea Stadium,

Schmidt told the media they were "comfortable" strikeouts. "I was right on every pitch," he said. "I just swung through the ball, that's all."

Danny Ozark remembered.

Ozark remembered Schmidt's tantalizing promise and all the maddening hours he spent trying to cajole the Phillies' future superstar along the roller coaster that was the 1973 season.

Ozark, a rookie manager barraged with heavy media flak . . . Schmidt, a rookie slugger who would bat .196 with 136 strikeouts in just 367 at-bats. The mix was as volatile as white phosphorous and water. It made for some of the most fascinating people-watching in the history of the franchise.

The Wizard of Oze is retired now, surrounded by those Vero Beach orange trees we used to joke about after his ballclub became the scourge of the National League, with Schmidt and Greg Luzinski spreading terror with their singing swords.

Danny and Ginny Ozark were watching on TV in their den Saturday afternoon when the magic moment arrived, when Schmidt ripped that heaven-sent 3–0 fastball to end his five-homer miniseries with a finish not even the most jaded Hollywood screenplay hack would have contrived.

For eighteen seasons, Mike Schmidt put on a power-hitting clinic while also playing a sure-handed third base.

"That's when I got goosebumbles all over my body," Ozark, still a world-class malaprop, said of Schmidt homer No. 500. "It couldn't have come at a nicer time or a better place than the park of the Pirates team that was the chief rival of the Phillies."

Yep, Ozark remembered saying during a moment of 1973 frustration. "I'd trade Schmitty for a wagonload of pumpkins."

He remembered the wheedling, the needling, the fatherly lectures of what a lot of people, including Schmidt, felt at the time was a heavy-handed approach to the future superstar.

And Ozark provided a fascinating postscript to the '73 season, a little-known event that unfolded in Veterans Stadium while the New York Mets and Oakland A's were battling in the World Series.

"What happened after that season, we brought him into Philadelphia, after the lousy year that he really had," Ozark remembered. "He was striking out and not really hitting that much. We called him up and brought him in before he went to Puerto Rico for winter baseball. He stayed with us in the batting cage for a week. He was quite reluctant to come. We worked at it but the first couple of days he didn't feel like doing anything—you know how Mike was about his feelings.

"The third day through Saturday he really worked at it—cripes, he hit an hour each day—and he went down to Puerto Rico and had a helluva winter. The next season he was a different hitter and just continued on hitting those home runs."

1978: ANOTHER DISAPPOINTMENT FOR YAZ

In all the long history of the Boston Red Sox, a history filled with bitter defeats, perhaps the worst was the October 2, 1978, loss to the New York Yankees in a one-game playoff mandated when the two teams finished the regular season tied. No one felt the loss more deeply than Carl Yastrzemski, who had played in two losing World Series (in 1967 and '75) and must have known he was running out of chances to be on a championship team. Peter Gammons told the sad story in the October 3, 1978, *Boston Globe.*

Carl Yastrzemski took one step toward first, stopped, and started to look away. But limply he turned back, to watch in fatal disbelief.

Rick Burleson pulled back to the third base bag, turned, and watched, too. So did Jerry Remy, standing on first. As they stood, frozen, Yankee catcher Thurman Munson waved his mask above his head, and Lou Piniella, his hands raised in triumph, started in from right field. And when the ball finally came down to Graig Nettles and he held it for all the world to see, the Yankees had tickets to a paradise called Kansas City and the Red Sox were going home.

When it was over, Yankee owner George Steinbrenner stood in the Red Sox clubhouse. "It's a shame that this is not the World Series, that our series is not seven games and when we're finished with each other that the season then isn't over," he said. "We are the two best teams in baseball. We said that on the field today. We won, but you didn't lose."

After an entire season that proved nothing except that the Red Sox and Yankees are equals, they tried to decide it all with one game. In a sense, it was a microcosm of the entire season: Boston leading, New York surging ahead, Boston rallying frantically—until, in the end, the difference was one run, a Boston runner watching, 90 feet from home, and enough ifs and maybes for every one of their games, enough for each winter's night ahead.

It was a split decision after 15 rounds between two proud, battered champions named Marciano and Ali, two teams worn to profound respect for one another.

But it was also Yankees 5, Red Sox 4, and the Yankees are the American League East champions, with the Red Sox second. In the end, it was another promise turned frustration that every New Englander has lived with since Harry Frazee sold Babe Ruth to New York. As historic a season, as magnificent a game, it was still the 1975 World Series, the 1967, 1949, '48 and '46. "We have everything in the world to be proud of," said Yastrzemski, "what we don't have is the ring."

Bucky Dent. This was a game that Rich Gossage saved by getting Jim Rice and Yastrzemski with Burleson and Remy on in the ninth. It began with Yaz hitting a stunning home run off Ron Guidry, with Guidry struggling through until the seventh with barely a hint of the fire that has made him 25–3. It was a game in which the winning run turned out to be a Reggie Jackson homer, a game that had Gossage bail out of two-on, one-out jams the last two innings, a game also saved by two memorable defensive plays by Lou Piniella, who is a winner.

But somehow this winter in a pub in East Cambridge or St. Alban's, Vt., or Somerset, Mass., someone will say, "Bucky Dent." Harry Brecheen, Denny Galehouse, Jim Lonborg's two days' rest, Jim Burton and Bucky Dent. The Yankee shortstop, batting because Willie Randolph is injured and Fred Stanley thus had to go in at second base, hit a three-run Fenway net job in the seventh that killed Mike Torrez' shutout and was the game's bottom line.

"They lose. We suffer," said The Boston Globe *after the Red Sox fell to Bucky Dent and the Yankees in the great 1978 playoff game. "We wait until next year and hope, despite all, that it will be different."*

Pitching on three days' rest, Guidry did not have the fastball that brought him one of the greatest seasons any pitcher has ever had. "He was throwing 85 percent sliders," said Fred Lynn. "He wasn't the same guy we saw earlier. I don't see how he could last throwing that way. His elbow will fall off."

Yastrzemski sat on a fastball and smashed it down the right-field line to lead off the second. But between then and Dent's homer, while the Red Sox hit a half dozen drives to the warning track and did manage a second run, they had chances and didn't capitalize.

George Scott lined a double off the base of the center-field wall in the third—helped by Mickey Rivers' lack of sunglasses (perhaps he didn't call the weather bureau to find out if the sun was out). And after Jack Brohamer bunted him to third for the first out, Burleson tapped to Nettles. Twenty-four times in the last month the Red Sox had a runner on third and failed to score him; five of those games they lost by one run.

In the sixth, Burleson doubled into the corner, Remy bunted him to third and Rice banged a single to center, his 139th RBI. But after a Yaz grounder and an intentional walk to Carlton Fisk came one of Piniella's two key plays.

Lynn was trying to go to left. Guidry gave him a breaking ball down and in, and Lynn drove it deep and to dead right field, to the foul pole side of the bullpen. "I don't hit five balls there all season," said Lynn. "I can't figure out why he was there." Asked, Piniella shrugged. "I don't really remember where I was playing him," he said. But turning away and near the warning track, he fought the brutal sun and made the catch. "Don't anyone ever tell me Piniella isn't a good outfielder," said Don Zimmer. "I've never seen the man make a mistake."

Guidry thus had survived the sixth down only 2–0, and Torrez went into the seventh with a two-hitter. Stuff? He had struck out Munson three times, which should say enough. With one out, Chris Chambliss singled through the hole to left, Roy White singled to center, Jim Spencer batted for Brian Doyle—whose replacement would be Stanley—and flied out. So Dent had to bat.

He fouled a ball off his foot, and it was there that Mickey Rivers and batboy Sandy Salandrea talked Dent into trying Rivers' bat. He did. "I thought I got the fastball in enough on him," said Torrez. "He kinda jerked back, and I never thought it would carry." Ah, a winter's lament—in the second inning the wind turned around. It had been blowing in from left.

Ah, a winter's irony: For all the complaints of the luck of the Fenway draw, Lynn's was a Yankee Stadium homer, Dent's (and, eventually, Jackson's) were Yankee Stadium outs.

Torrez then walked Rivers on a 3–2 pitch, and Zimmer yanked him. Ah, a winter's second guessing: Torrez says he was throwing well, had fanned Munson thrice and shouldn't have left. Relief pitchers' records show Dick Drago a better man with men on base than Bob Stanley. "Stanley had done the job all year," said Zimmer. He came in, Rivers stole second, and Munson doubled to left-center for another run.

Gossage came on when Scott singled with one out in the seventh, and Jackson's drive into the center-field bleachers off Stanley made it 5–2 in the eighth. The game-winner. "I'm just a guy who always ends up in the right place at the right time," said Reggie.

Gossage, with a 5–2 lead, began struggling. Remy—whose brilliant day included two hits, a perfect bunt and a diving stop—doubled and rode home on Yastrzemski's single. Fisk fouled off four two-strike pitches and singled, and Lynn lined another single to left for another run. Gossage got out of that inning when Butch Hobson flied out and he pumped a fastball past George Scott, but a one-out walk to Burleson began trouble in the ninth.

Remy hit a line drive toward Piniella in right. Piniella never saw it. Momentarily, even as third base coach Eddie Yost frantically waved him around, Burleson thought Piniella could catch it, held up. And still the play wasn't over.

If Piniella had been unlucky, the ball would have shot by him on the hop, rolled to the bullpen, Burleson would have scored and Remy, the winning run, would have been on third. "I went to where I thought it would land," said Piniella. "I saw it when it hit and reacted." The play was like Rogatien Vachon flicking his glove out for a screen shot, and Burleson was kept at second. On third, he would have scored on Rice's fly. Instead, he was on third, two outs. Gossage, Yastrzemski. Fastball pitcher, fastball hitter. "I wasn't going to mess around with breaking junk and get beaten by anything but my best," said Gossage. "Yastrzemski's the greatest player I've ever played against. I just wound up and threw it as hard as I could. I couldn't tell you where."

All of the thirty-nine-year-old Carl Yastrzemski's efforts were in vain in 1978.

Yastrzemski thought the 1–0 pitch would tail away. It tailed in. He tried to hold up. He went through. The ball sailed high into foul territory off third, and Yastrzemski took one step, stopped and started to look away.

When it was over, Jackson sat in the Boston clubhouse. "Both of us should be champions," he told Scott.

"Win it all," Yastrzemski said, embracing him, as across the way Catfish Hunter prepared to take Ken Harrelson's lucky hat the rest of the way through Kansas City and the World Series, if the anti-climax doesn't get them.

Jackson and Steinbrenner came by to tell the Red Sox what they themselves would like to believe: that the best team in baseball is better than the second best team in baseball by a run with a runner on third in the 163rd game of the season.

Which is true, and perhaps it is consolation enough. For New England has seen the Red Sox one run down, a runner on third, the seventh game of the Series before. It was one of the great games in the history of the grand old game, but it was the ultimate Red Sox fan's frustration.

But as New England is conservative and the conservative's ethic is that man's lot can never truly be enhanced, perhaps in the end the Olde Towne Teame has given its faithful what will comfort them most in the cold days and long nights until they meet again, in Winter Haven.

1978: CARLTON FISK'S KINGDOM

When Carlton Fisk ended his career in 1993, he had amassed Hall of Fame credentials, including breaking Bob Boone's major league record of 2225 games caught. This excerpt from Melissa Ludtke's "The Despot and the Diplomat," published in the April 10, 1978, *Sports Illustrated,* captures Fisk—and his brethren—in all their irascible glory.

Right and overleaf: In his record-setting twenty-four-year career with the Red Sox and White Sox, Carlton Fisk always spoke his mind.

Catchers and home-plate umpires are almost certainly the oddest of all sport's odd couples. Crouching and sweating together beneath layers of padding and suffering like bruises from foul tips and curves in the dirt, they play a game within a game, one in which other players are seldom involved. The catcher acts as his team's diplomat, his words usually as guarded and as subtly delivered as his signs to the pitcher. The umpire is an autocrat, often congenial, sometimes unyielding. However, the peace between the diplomat and the benevolent despot is tenuous and often destroyed. When this happens, their masks fly, and what began as a discussion inaudible to virtually everyone else in the park becomes as much of a show as an Ali weigh-in. That's exactly what happened one day late last season when Umpire Don Denkinger miscalled the first pitch of a game.

Red Sox catcher Carlton Fisk caught that pitch, a fastball, after it crossed the middle of the plate.

"Ball one," said Denkinger.

Fisk, outraged and astounded, leaped straight up, hitting Denkinger under the chin with his catcher's helmet. "How in hell can you call that a ball?" he screamed.

"Take it easy! Take it easy!" Denkinger said.

"You're in for a bleep day if you keep calling pitches like that," said Fisk.

"It's the first pitch. What do you want to do? Hang me?"

"The first pitch. If I let you get away with that, the entire afternoon will be awful."

"So I blew it," said Denkinger. "Relax. I know I missed it."

"You sure as hell did miss it. And I'm jumping on you simply to wake you up."

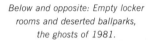

Below and opposite: Empty locker rooms and deserted ballparks, the ghosts of 1981.

1981: "THE SILENCE"

For any baseball fan, 1981 was a year to forget. That was the season of the players' strike that stretched for fifty long days, followed by the one-time institution of a bizarre split-season system in an attempt to reignite fan interest. Though other lockouts and strikes occurred both before and after this one, no event in the history of baseball has demonstrated so starkly the vulnerability of the great game—or, as Roger Angell showed in his 1981 "The Silence," reprinted from *Late Innings* (1988), how much we would lose if baseball disappeared forever.

Last week, my wife and I came uptown late one night in a cab after having dinner with friends of ours in the Village. We wheeled through the warm and odorous light-strewn summer dark on the same northward route home we have followed hundreds of times over the years, I suppose: bumping and lurching up Sixth non-stop, with the successive gateways of staggered green lights magically opening before us, and the stately tall street lights (if you tipped your head back on the cab seat and watched them upside down through the back window of the cab: I had drunk a bit of wine) forming a narrowing golden archway astern; and then moving more quietly through the swerves and small hills of the Park, where the weight and silence of the black trees wrapped us in a special summer darkness. The cabdriver had his radio on, and the blurry sounds of the news—the midnight news, I suppose—passed over us there in the back seat, mixing with the sounds of the wind coming in through the open cab windows, and the motion of our ride, and the whole sense of city night. All was as always, I mean, except that now it came to me, unsurprisingly at first but then with a terrific jolt of unhappiness and mourning, that this radio news was altered for there was no baseball in it. Without knowing it, I had been waiting for those other particular sounds, for that other part of the summer night, but it was missing, of course—no line scores, no winning and losing pitchers, no homers and highlights, no records approached or streaks cut short, no "Meanwhile, over in the National League," no double-zip early innings from Anaheim or Chavez Ravine, no Valenzuela and no Rose, no Goose and no Tom, no Yaz, no Mazz, no nothing.

The strike by this time was more than a week old, and I had so far sustained the shock of it and the change of it with more fortitude and patience than I had expected of myself. The issues seemed far removed from me—too expensive or too complicated, for some reason, for me to hold them clearly in my mind for long, although I am an attentive and patient fan. I would wait, then, with whatever composure I could find, until it was settled, days or weeks from now, and in some fashion or other I would fill up the empty eveningtimes and morningtimes I had once spent (I did not say "wasted"; I would never say "wasted") before the tube and with the sports pages. It might even be better for me to do without baseball for a while, although I could not imagine why. All this brave nonsense was knocked out of me in an instant, there in the cab, and suddenly the loss of that murmurous little ribbon of baseball-by-radio, the ordinary news of the game, seemed to explain a lot of things about the much larger loss we fans are all experiencing because of the strike. The refrain of late-night baseball scores; the sounds of the televised game from the next room (the room empty, perhaps, for the moment, but the game running along in there just the same and quietly waiting for us to step in and rejoin it when we are of a mind to); the mid-game mid-event from some car or cab that pulls up beside us for a few seconds in traffic before the light changes; the baseball conversation in the elevator that goes away when two men get off together at the eleventh floor, taking the game with them; the flickery white fall of light on our hands and arms and the scary sounds of the crowd that suddenly wake us up, in bed or in the study armchair, where we have fallen asleep, with the set and the game still on—all these streams and continuities, it seems to me, are part of the greater, riverlike flow of baseball. No other sport, I think, conveys anything like this sense of cool depth and fluvial steadiness, and when you stop for a minute and think about the game it is easy to see why this should be so. The slow, inexorable progression of baseball events—balls and strikes, outs and innings, batters stepping up and batters being retired, pitchers and sides changing on the field, innings turning into games and games into series, and all these merging and continuing, in turn, in the box scores and the averages and the slowly fluctuous standings—are what make the game quietly and uniquely satisfying. Baseball flows past us all through the summer—it is one of the reasons that summer exists—and wherever we happen to stand on its green banks we can sense with only a glance across its shiny expanse that the long, unhurrying swirl and down-flowing have their own purpose and direction, that the river is headed, in its own sweet time, toward a downsummer broadening and debouchment and to its end in the estuary of October.

River people, it is said, count on the noises and movement of nearby water, even without knowing it, and feel uneasy and unaccountably diminished if they must move away for a while and stay among plains inhabitants. That is almost the way it is for us just now, but it is worse than that, really, because this time it is the river that has gone away—just stopped—and all of us who live along these banks feel a fretful sense of loss and a profound disquiet over the sudden cessation of our reliable old stream. The main issue of the baseball strike, I have read, concerns the matter of compensation for owners who have lost a player to free agency, but when this difficulty is resolved and the two sides come to an agreement (as they will someday), what compensation can ever be made to us, the fans, who are the true owners and neighbors and keepers of the game, for this dry, soundless summer and for the loss of our joy?

1984: THE CUBS ALMOST MAKE IT

The N.L. counterpart to the Red Sox—a team with a tremendously colorful and varied history, but no World Series rings in too many years—is the Chicago Cubs. Few fans are prouder or more devout than Cubs fans, but they've had remarkably little to cheer about over the years: Not a single appearance in the Series since 1945. In 1984, the Cubs almost made it again, taking a two-games-to-none lead over the San Diego Padres in the NLCS (then a best-of-five series). But as novelist Barry Gifford writes in *Basepaths: The Best of the Minneapolis Review of Baseball* (1991), they failed bitterly yet again, overcome by bad luck, their own blunders, and Steve Garvey's superb hitting.

Steve Garvey, who played with remarkable consistency for nineteen years and always looked good doing it.

The Cubs won the first game of the National League playoffs by an astounding score of thirteen to nothing, the most lopsided contest in the history of postseason play, including the World Series. In addition to setting a new record for most home runs in one playoff game, the Cubs established new National League marks for hits (sixteen), runs in an inning (six), runs in a game and, in a more esoteric vein, the number of men facing a pitcher in one inning (twelve). Perhaps the most remarkable statistic is that each Cub player in the starting lineup had at least one hit and one run batted in; the combined Cub batting average for the game was .421 (also a National League record).

This auspicious debut was followed by a second Cub victory, this time by a more modest count of four to two. All they needed was one more win to do away with thirty-nine years of failure. It would have to be done, however, in San Diego.

In his final *Newsletter* of the season, a supplement to the *Baseball Abstract*, Bill James wrote—three weeks or so prior to the National League playoffs—that the Padres seemed to have the edge over the Cubs should they meet in the championship series, but that the Cubs were a "heck of a team." The Pads, James said, would have to beat Rick Sutcliffe at least once in order to take the pennant in what was likely to be one of the best league playoffs of all time. My hat, if I wore one, would at this moment be off to Mr. James.

For a while it looked like San Diego wouldn't have another shot at Sutcliffe, but they knocked off the Cubs in style, seven to one, in the first game back at Jack Murphy Stadium. My daughter Phoebe and I went down to San Diego for Game Four, certain that the Padres had had their brief flurry of success, that Scott Sanderson would administer the coup de grace, saving Sutcliffe for the opening World Series game against Detroit, which had wiped out Kansas City in three straight. . . .

We got much more—and much less—than we bargained for. Game Four turned out to be Steve "Call Me Senator" Garvey's Impossible Dream. In the battle of "our" ex-Dodger versus "their" ex-Dodger, Garvey stroked two singles, a double and the game winning two-run homer in the bottom of the ninth, driving in five of San Diego's seven runs; Garvey's counterpart, Ron Cey, who had piled up a club leading ninety-seven RBI during the regular season, stranded seven baserunners during an oh-for-five that included four pop-ups and a weak ground-out to second with the bases loaded in the ninth. It was a great game and the greatest post-season single game performance by a player since Reggie Jackson's three homer show that put LA away for keeps in 1977. Now the Cubs were forced to shoot the works with Sutcliffe.

Chicago, 1984—a season of spectacular successes that went on just three games too long.

Phoebe and I watched Game Five on television. She was confident the Cubs would come through; after all, she'd been born and raised in California, land of sunshine and optimism, the New World. I wasn't so sure; I had that Old Cub feeling and I couldn't shake it. I kept seeing in my mind a sign a Padre fan had held up the night before in Illinois Governor Jim Thompson's face: 39 MORE YEARS.

What happened in Game Five is public knowledge: After staking Sutcliffe to a three to nothing lead after two innings, the Cubs blew it. Manager Jim Frey left Sutcliffe in too long but that wasn't the only crucial factor. Durham made a critical error on a ground ball, Sandberg had a sure double play hopper off the bat of Tony Gwynn take a crazy leap over his head that went for two bases, Cey went oh-for-four and stranded four more runners; and Steve Garvey, named Most Valuable Player of the series, knocked in the final nail with a single up the middle to lock up the game for the Padres, six to three. It was their first title in the sixteen years of their existence, and they deserved it. Bill James was right: San Diego beat Rick Sutcliffe when they had to and it had been a great series, one of the best.

Walking out of Jack Murphy Stadium on Saturday night, after Garvey's off-field blast had guaranteed tomorrow for the Pads, I took a close look at Padre fans celebrating around me. They were mostly well-groomed, tanned, healthy looking people,

Opposite: In an early incarnation as a starter, Dennis Eckersley helped carry the Cubs to the 1984 division championship but couldn't overcome the Padres in the NLCS.

Southern Californians. If the Padres lost the playoffs they could say, "Okay, it's too bad, but it's been a great season," and look forward to a "winter" of windsurfing and sailboats. But what about the Cub fans? If the Cubs lost, all they had to look forward to was wearing galoshes and parkas and hats with flaps over their ears to ward off "The Hawk," the bitter Chicago winter wind, while they waited at snow-swept streetcorners for busses that never arrive. Without that inner warmth, the glow that comes from knowing the Cubs had finally come home a winner, the wait could be unbearable.

"You spend thirty years in this game, and you get good and damn disappointed," said Dallas Green. "But this ranks the hell up there with any of 'em." Goose Gossage, the San Diego relief pitcher who had saved the pennant-winning game, understood. "The whole world is shocked right now," Gossage said in the victor's clubhouse. "The whole world was rooting for the Cubs."

IN PRAISE OF STATISTICS

One of the unexpected baseball growth industries of the 1980s and '90s was the burgeoning use and study of statistics. Fueled by the popularity of Rotisserie League Baseball and other fantasy games, statistics are analyzed by such organizations as the Society for American Baseball Research (SABR) for more serious purpose: To find the truth that lies behind long-accepted baseball truisms and, in doing so, evaluate players' performances in a truly objective manner. The following, from John Thorn and Pete Palmer's *The Hidden Game of Baseball* (1984), provided the young discipline's raison d'être.

The hidden game is played with statistics (and, it could be said, by them), but it extends beyond the record books. One enters the game whenever one attempts to evaluate performance, which is possible only through comparison, implied or explicit. How good a hitter is Eddie Murray? How would Rogers Hornsby do if he were active today? Why can't the Red Sox get themselves some decent starting pitchers? What value does Oakland receive from Rickey Henderson's stolen bases? When is an intentional base on balls advisable? The answers to these and countless other questions are of concern to those who play the hidden game. . . .

In the eternal Hot Stove League, statistics stand in for their creators, and the better the statistics, the more "real" (i.e., reasonable) the results. In recent years baseball's already copious traditional stats have been supplemented, though not supplanted, by a variety of new formulations—some of them official, like the save and the game winning RBI, most of them outlaws, like Runs Created or Total Average, though not without adherents. And with the explosion of new stats has come an outspoken antistatistical camp, with the two sides aligning themselves along battle lines that were drawn almost at the dawn of baseball.

The antis might argue that baseball is an elementally simple game: pitch, hit, run, throw, catch—what else is there that matters? Playing it or watching it is deeply satisfying without examination of any sort, let along rigorous statistical analysis. So why do we need new stats? Don't we have enough ways to measure performance? Don't we have *too many*? Why subject every incident on the field to such maniacal ledger-book accounting?

How can baseball's beauty fail to wither under the glare of intense mathematical scrutiny? For those of an antistatistical bent, baseball, like a butterfly, is poetry in motion and a cold, dead thing when pinned to the page. If we subject the game to ever more intricate analysis, in hope that it will yield up its mysteries, are we not breaking the butterfly upon a wheel, in Pope's phrase?

For the statistician, too, baseball is indeed like a butterfly, whose grace can be glimpsed while it is in flight . . . but then it is gone, having scarcely registered upon the memory. One doesn't truly know any longer what it looked like, where it came from, how it vanished in an instant. The butterfly's coloring, its detail, cannot be absorbed while it is in flight; it must be examined to appreciate its complexity. One may love its simplicity in flight as one may love the simplicity of baseball while standing in the outfield or sitting in the grandstand. But the complex texture of the game, which for many is its real delight—the thing that pleases the mind as well as the eye—cannot be fully grasped while the game is in progress.

And that's what statistical analysis allows us to do. Statistics are not the instruments of vivisection, taking the life out of a thing in order to examine it; rather, statistics are themselves the vital part of baseball, the only tangible and imperishable remains of games played yesterday or a hundred years ago.

Baseball may be loved without statistics, but it cannot be understood without them. Statistics are what make baseball a sport rather than a spectacle, what make its past worthy of our interest as well as its present.

OCTOBER 15, 1986: COLD DINNERS

Of all the games yet played in the history of the NLCS, the most suspenseful, most unlikely, and most memorable of all may have been the sixth game of the 1986 series between the New York Mets and the Houston Astros. Leading three games to two, but terrified of facing Mike Scott (who had already stifled them twice) in a seventh game, the Mets came back from a three-run deficit in the ninth inning to tie Game Six; went ahead by a run in the 14th, only to see the Astros tie it on a home run by Billy Hatcher; scored three runs in the top of the sixteenth; and finally won 7–6 when Jesse Orosco struck out Kevin Bass with the tying and go-ahead runs on base. In a piece published in the *New York Post* two days later, Maury Allen was still breathless.

> In a quarter of a century of baseball coverage, from the Original Mets of 1962 to the Unbelievable Mets of 1986, I have never seen a game like Game 6 of the just completed NLCS. Has anybody?
>
> It is more than 24 hours later, and the plays and the players shift through my mind: Len Dykstra coming off the bench and whacking a monstrous triple to center to wake his sleeping mates, Alan Ashby incredibly blowing a squeeze bunt in the first inning, a play so big it was lost in the confusion; Darryl Strawberry hitting a Dome-high popup that threatened the roof while the turf under centerfielder Billy Hatcher's feet turned to quicksand.
>
> There was the sight of Bob Knepper, the Houston lefthander who had pitched eight scoreless innings, squeezing the metal dugout bars in frustration from the ninth inning through Kevin Bass' 16th inning strikeout.

*The Mets were terrified of having to
face Mike Scott (right) in Game
Seven. But thanks to the clutch
play of Jesse Orosco (opposite) and
others, they didn't have to.*

Lenny Dykstra piles on as the Mets celebrate their stunning sixteen-inning victory over the Astros in the 1986 NLCS. "I'm just going to go somewhere and hide," Astros' outfielder Billy Hatcher said after the game. "I don't want to watch no more baseball."

Opposite: Everyone tried to console Donnie Moore (left) after he gave up a crucial home run in the '86 ALCS—but nothing helped.

As the innings passed into history, and the beauty of baseball was glorified by an infinite clock, Mike Scott sat on the Houston bench. He was a quietly menacing figure, professorial in his glasses, intimidating in his possibilities, the man who would keep the Mets from the pennant in another day.

The consensus had been almost unarguably Mets in six or Astros in seven. It would be Scott joining Mickey Lolich and Bob Gibson and Lew Burdette and Bill Dineen and Christy Mathewson as three-game winners in post-season play.

The tension in the Astrodome showed everywhere: on the parading players, on the Met bench, on the Houston players in and out of their clubhouse, on the fans fighting nature's call because the drama was too intense to miss, on the observers in the press box straining for some hint of an end and a peg on which to hang their reports of this Gothic confrontation.

A day later, in my neighborhood grocery store, at the dry cleaners, at the Post Office, at the bank, people begged for more details of the event. Everyone hungered for more tidbits.

"It was five o'clock," my wife said, "and nobody moved from the office. They just forgot to go home. They just listened and listened and listened."

There were cold dinners in Westchester and in Queens, on Staten Island and Long Island, in The Bronx and the Battery and on Bedford Avenue in Brooklyn, where they thought they would never again care. Oh, how they cared!

On May 31, 1964, the Mets lost to the Giants in 23 innings at the Polo Grounds, and I remember how Bennett Cerf and John Charles Daley came on the air for "What's My Line?" and discussed the game. The audience tuned out that show and tuned in the ballgame.

There have been dozens of games in the last 25 years that have filled me with unbridled excitement, tension and awe at their magnificence. There was Bucky Dent lofting his Fenway Park homer in '78. There was Chris Chambliss fighting his way through surging fans at Yankee Stadium after his '76 pennant winner against the Royals. There was Carlton Fisk, waving desperately for his drive to left to stay fair for the Game 6 win in 12 breathless innings in Boston in '75.

Tom Seaver kept us breathless in July of '69 with 8 1/3 perfect innings against the Cubs. Jim Bunning threw half-a-dozen curveballs in a row before he could get John Stephenson for the 27th out of his Father's Day perfect game in '64. Jim Hickman scraped the overhanging Polo Grounds scoreboard to end Roger Craig's 18-game losing streak in '63. Roger Maris battled the ghost of Babe Ruth with courageous effort in Game 154 of the '61 season, hitting No. 59 that game and missing the tying No. 60 with three huge drives.

But nothing could touch Wednesday's endless drama. Inning after inning with the pennant riding—forget that it was the sixth game; just remember the Mets were scared to death of Scott—unbearable tension, endless thrills.

I wanted it to go on forever.

"NOTHING TO FORGIVE"

New York and Houston didn't play the only memorable championship series in 1986. The Boston Red Sox and California Angels' series was also one of the most dramatic in history, with Game Five standing out as the turning point. The Angels led the series three games to one and were one strike away from winning the championship when Boston's Dave Henderson hit a two-run home run off relief ace Donnie Moore. The Sox won that game, destroyed the demoralized Angels in the next two, and won the series.

But the effects on Donnie Moore of the Angels' Game Five loss reached far beyond the bounds of baseball. As Thomas Boswell writes in "Nothing to Forgive," reprinted from his 1990 collection *Game Day,* the impact of that one pitch calls into question the standards to which we hold our sports heroes.

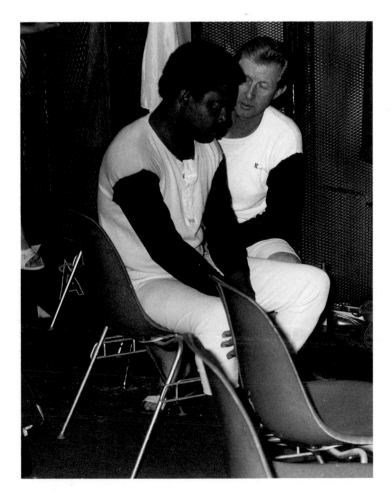

This is for Bill Buckner, Ralph Branca, John McNamara, Tom Niedenfuer, Don Denkinger, Johnny Pesky and Gene Mauch. It's for the '64 Phillies, the '78 Red Sox, the '87 Blue Jays and every Cub since World War II. In particular, it's for Donnie Moore, who shot his wife, then committed suicide this week.

You, and countless others who get branded as "goats" in sports, didn't do anything wrong. We know it, though we almost never say it. Just once, let's put it in words: The reason we don't forgive you is because there's nothing to forgive in the first place. You tried your best and failed. In games, there's a law that says somebody has to lose.

Many of us wish that, just once, we could be in your shoes and have a chance to fail so grandly. Although, if we really had to live the experience and its aftermath, which sometimes lasts a lifetime, maybe we would not.

Bill Buckner was a fine ballplayer for more than two decades, but may always be best remembered for his World Series error in 1986.

We've had our share of sad stories in sports recently. But none approaches Donnie Moore's. Numerous other athletes who're in trouble—taking heat, answering tough questions, hearing catcalls—got themselves in hot water by doing what they knew was wrong. All Moore did was pitch despite a sore arm, throw a nice nasty knee-high forkball and watch it sail over the left-field fence.

Nobody will ever be able to prove that the haunting memory of giving up Dave Henderson's home run in the 1986 American League playoffs led Moore to commit suicide. Maybe, someday, we'll learn about some other possible cause. But, right now, what some people are saying, and many are thinking, is that this "goat" business isn't funny anymore.

Moore was a good little pitcher, a battler, a student of the game, a tough guy with a sensitive inside who was one of Mauch's favorite players. That tells a lot, because Mauch respects Joe DiMaggio and about two other people.

For two seasons, late in his twelve-year career, Moore became a star. He came within one foul tick of pitching the California Angels into their only World Series. But Henderson, off balance, barely tipped the two-strike pitch. With the next swing, Henderson made history. He kept the Red Sox alive so that they could go to the World Series in the Angels' place—and endure miseries.

"Ever since he gave up the home run . . . he was never himself again," said Dave Pinter, Moore's agent for twelve years. "He blamed himself for the Angels not going to the World Series. He constantly talked about the Henderson home run. . . . I tried to get him to go to a psychiatrist, but he said, 'I don't need it. I'll get over it.'. . . That home run killed him."

"You destroyed a man's life over one pitch," exploded the Angels' Brian Downing. "The guy was just not the same after that. . . . He was never treated fairly. He wasn't given credit for all the good things he did. . . . Nobody was sympathetic. I never, ever saw him be credited for getting us to the playoffs, because all you ever heard about, all you ever read about was one pitch."

Moore's wife, Tonya, once said that, after the Pitch, Moore would often come home after games at Anaheim Stadium, where he was booed, and burst into tears.

One of the powerful appeals of sports is its artificially created fairness. Every precaution is taken to ensure a level playing field. In a sense, sports is purely democratic. Almost nothing about you, except the way you play the game, is inspected or judged.

That's why sports are, in a sense, an escape. All the moral ambiguities of daily life are suspended. Somebody wins and is happy. Somebody loses, but gets to play again the next day or season.

Duane Thomas once said, "If the Super Bowl is the 'ultimate game,' why do they play it again next year?" The answer is: "So somebody else can win it. And so whoever loses this year doesn't feel too bad."

Some people get over losing their "ultimate game." Perhaps no manager ever made a bigger blunder than Tommy Lasorda when he had Niedenfuer pitch to Jack Clark with first base open and the Dodgers just one out from reaching the World Series. Clark hit a three-run homer and St. Louis went to the Series—which they lost because of—no, we're not going to blame Denkinger today.

Lasorda wept in the clubhouse, went to the players to apologize, then went on with his life.

At the moment he manages the reigning world champions. Maybe Lasorda coped so well because he'd already gone to three Series and won one.

The flaw in our attitude—perhaps it is even an American predisposition with Puritan roots—is to equate defeat with sin. The unspoken assumption is that those who lose must do so because of some moral flaw.

Johnny Pesky, a World Series "goat" in 1946.

Sports, especially pro sports, is not a morality play, much as it suits our national appetite to act as if it were. Even some athletes, perhaps including Moore, seem to ·crush themselves under a burden of self-imposed guilt in areas of life where no cause for guilt exists.

If you work hard enough, sacrifice enough, then you win. That's what many coaches teach. Or should we say preach? It might be more honest, and healthier, to say that if you work very hard you will become excellent, and because of that excellence, you may do great deeds and win great prizes. Unless, of course, you don't. Because, sometimes, the other player is better or luckier. In which case you simply have to be satisfied with your excellence and the dignity of your effort.

Those of us who are merely fans and critics have a responsibility, too. The right to a raspberry comes with the price of a ticket and the right to an opinion goes with the First Amendment.

Still, before we boo or use words like "choke" and "goat," perhaps we should think sometimes of Donnie Moore.

NOLAN RYAN: THE ARC OF A CAREER

Nothing about Nolan Ryan, who retired at the end of the 1993 season, astounds more than his longevity. Not his remarkable competitiveness, almost always masked by an even-tempered demeanor. Not his 324 wins, his 5714 strikeouts, his seven no-hitters (thrown in three different decades, with the last two taking place after Ryan was more than forty years old), his clear passage into the Hall of Fame. His longevity: Twenty-seven years of pitching stretching from 1966 to 1993.

How long did Nolan Ryan pitch? When he made his first appearance with the Mets in 1966, Hall of Famers Johnny Bench, Rod Carew, and Tom Seaver (all of whom had careers lasting fifteen years or longer, and all of whom have been retired at least seven years) had not yet played an inning of major league baseball. Mickey Mantle, Ernie Banks, Roberto Clemente, Sandy Koufax, and Whitey Ford were still active. Yogi Berra and Warren Spahn had retired just the year before. Ken Griffey, Jr., Frank Thomas, Roberto Alomar, and Gary Sheffield hadn't been born yet.

For a generation of baseball fans, Nolan Ryan was always there—moving from team to team (though often and appropriately, it seemed, landing in home-state Texas). The following excerpts take a quick look at three phases of his career: The beginnings, the first big year, and the pitcher's plans for a graceful exit.

"A Little White Lie"
From Jerome Holtzman, *Baseball Digest* (August 1991)

The Nolan Ryan story starts with Red Murff.

"In 1963, I began working for the New York Mets as a scout after a time with the Houston Colt .45s," Murff recalled. "One Saturday morning, the first weekend in March, I was scouting in Galveston.

"As it happened, I had about an hour to pass on my way from Galveston to another scouting assignment that afternoon in Houston. So I figured I'd watch a high school baseball tournament in Alvin just to see who was winning.

"There was just one scout there—Mickey Sullivan, who worked for the Phillies. It was the second or third inning, and I didn't even know who was playing. Mickey told

Opposite: Portrait of the pitcher as a young man: Incomparable stuff, frighteningly uncertain control.

me it was Alvin High playing somebody, Clear Lake or Clear Creek. The Alvin coach was changing pitchers just about the time I got settled in.

"This skinny, handsome right-hander threw two fastballs, and I was thunderstruck. You could hear that ball explode. Then he threw an atrocious curveball, and the hitter doubled to right-center.

"'Who's that kid out there?' I asked Mickey Sullivan.

"'Nolan Ryan,' he answered. 'He doesn't have much, does he?'

"'I don't know,' I said. Then I started to bite my tongue. 'He doesn't have a very good curveball,' I added. That's the closest I've ever come to being a liar. That night, I went to the old Colt Stadium and saw Turk Farrell of Houston and Jim Maloney of the Cincinnati Reds pitch against each other in the twilight. They could both throw 95-mile-an-hour fastballs.

"At high noon, that young man I had seen threw harder than either of them. I'm a hunter and I know something about ballistics, and when I filled out my report for the Mets, I said that Ryan was in the 100-mile-an-hour range, that his fastball stayed level in flight, rose as it got to the plate, then exploded."

"Warning: Nolan Ryan's Smoke Is Dangerous to a Batter's Health"
From Arnold Hano, *Sport* (June 1973)

Take your Gaylord Perrys, and their carefully controlled sweat glands; your Mickey Lolichs, and the canny way they set up batters; your fatly indefatigable Wilbur Woods. You are not reminded, by any of these, of Sandy Koufax.

But then there is Nolan Ryan, the pride of the California Angels, manager Bobby Winkles' loveliest tiddly-wink, the stickpin that holds the American League franchise to the map of Anaheim. Nolan Ryan is to Anaheim what Steve Carlton is to Philadelphia, a marvelous pitcher on a team that gives him (a) few runs, or (b) none.

Ryan throws baseballs swifter than anyone since Sandy Koufax—swifter, even, than Sam McDowell. I tell you all this, because many do not know Nolan Ryan, and others know of him, but do not really know him.

I remember the day Bob Feller pitched in the 1939 All-Star game—bear with some nostalgia—and what Feller threw that day in Yankee Stadium was not a baseball but a pitcher of cream. That is how it looked from the rightfield bleachers, a thin stream of cream etching the sweet afternoon, and splashing untouched into the catcher's glove, as Johnny Mize and Dolf Camilli futilely tried to splatter some of that cream against their bats. Since that day I have not seen anyone except Nolan Ryan throw a baseball with that shocking speed—or at least regularly throw that fast. Jim Maloney could match that speed, but just for an inning or two; Koufax on his very greatest days only. Ryan throws like that all the time, more or less.

Ryan has more than speed. He is wild, an erratic fielder, a man unable to keep men close to base or pick them off. He led all of baseball's pitchers in strikeouts last year with 329—fourth highest in big-league history—and he led all of baseball's pitchers in walks, with 157, and he uncorked 18 wild pitches, which led the league, and he hit ten batters. You know what? All that wildness helps. He has them sweating at the plate, all the Sal Bandos (Ryan singles out Bando as the man he most enjoys pitching against) and the Harmon Killebrews of the world, the men with their bludgeons turned childishly weak by the realization a baseball may come out of Ryan's right hand, sailing upstairs at a murderous speed with an innocent disregard for direction.

Nolan Ryan wouldn't hit a man deliberately, but he says he'll brush back his best friend. Since no batter is his friend, you can imagine how he treats his enemies. "I've broken a few bones," he says, with a schoolboy smile. Besides the smile, he has dark, heavy, lugubrious eyebrows that turn his face into a contradictory cartoon—the smiling mourner, the mournful toothpaste ad. He's also six-foot-two, 195 pounds, rawboned at the shoulders, thick at the thigh and 26 years old last January 31, a star dawning in the Age of Aquarius.

"I don't remember the last time I got through a day without feeling some discomfort," Nolan Ryan wrote in 1992, but somehow he overcame his aches and pains to pitch for twenty-seven seasons.

But never mind his horoscope or his facial contradiction. It's that other contradiction we're interested in—pitching artistry and wildness. Ryan won 19 games last year and lost 16, and there are those who would tell you he'd have won four or five or even six more had he better control. Walks beat him, wild pitches beat him, stolen bases beat him, his throwing errors beat him. But if he had better control, they'd take deeper toeholds, and Harmon Killebrew wouldn't have made the impossible threat: "If he ever hits me with a fastball, I'll have him arrested for manslaughter." (Your next of kin, you mean, Harmon.) Reggie Jackson says, "He's the only man in baseball I'm afraid of."

"When It's Over"
From Nolan Ryan with Jerry Jenkins, *Miracle Man* (1992)

I don't sit around reflecting on my career, and I probably never will. The reason I don't now is because I'm still in it. I don't want to live in the past. I get a lot of satisfaction out of what I have accomplished and knowing that it's brought joy to people, but when it's over, I'll just move on.

One thing I don't want to do is wait until I can't get the ball to the plate before I know it's time to hang it up. It's a bitter pill to swallow when you realize you can't get the job done any longer, and every player handles it differently. You see a lot of guys retire and live off the glow of that until it wears off, then they want to make a comeback. They watch television and they think they can hit the new pitchers or get out the new hitters. It's sad to see them try to come back. You'll never see me doing that. Once I decide it's over, it'll be over.

I can say I want to be prepared to deal with how much I'll miss the game, but I suppose it's like thinking you're prepared for a loved one's death. There's no doubt in my mind that I'll miss baseball a lot. You don't have something dominate your life this long and then walk away from it without regrets.

People are always asking me if I think about the Hall of Fame. I really don't, and I hope people know me well enough by now to know that I'm being truthful. The subject is brought up more and more each year as guys younger than me are being elected. People used to debate whether I'd make it. Now they pretty much assume I will. I don't think about it one way or the other. I believe you can only control what you can control, and since Hall of Famers are chosen by people voting, I'll leave it at that. If they think I'm deserving, I'll make it. If they don't, I won't.

I can live with that. Either way, I'll always be able to look in the mirror and know that the guy looking back gave the game and the fans and his ball club everything he had to give for as long as he could.

1993: GEORGE BRETT SAYS GOODBYE

Has there ever been a ballplayer who seemed to love the game more than George Brett? Almost from the moment he arrived in Kansas City, a highly touted prospect expected to solve the Royals' third-base problems, he captured fans' hearts with his ebullient manner, high spirits, and boundless self-confidence. And, of course, he could play.

Could he ever play. During the twenty-one-year career that ended in 1993, Brett hit over .300 eleven times, including an astonishing .390 in 1980 (the highest batting average since Ted Williams's famous .406 in 1941). Add to those gaudy numbers 3154 hits, 317 home runs, 201 stolen bases, more than 1500 runs scored and batted in, and far more walks than strikeouts, and you have one of the most multitalented stars of recent years—and a certain first-ballot selection to the Hall of Fame.

As Gib Twyman's September 26, 1993, article in the *Kansas City Star* shows, Brett's retirement announcement was a graceful encapsulation of his whole career.

The shirt told you all you needed to know about what was going on inside George Brett as he went from No. 5 to 9 to 5.

The shirt was the thing touching his heart, and it was soaked with so much emotion and perspiration it looked as if George had punctuated his 21-year major-league career by jumping into the Kauffman Stadium fountains.

Those feelings came pouring out of Brett as he dived right into the uncharted waters of retirement.

"I'm sweating a little. I was under some stress up there," Brett said.

"I had been feeling calm and relaxed all day," he added, a catch suddenly in his voice.

He was doing better than a long-time runnin' buddy, Jamie Quirk. Two or three times, Quirk tried to get going in a TV interview. He never really quite made it. Tears came. He brushed them away. They came some more. His voice cracked over and over. "He's just very special," Quirk finally said, hardly forming the words.

It was that kind of moment Saturday as Brett told us he was hanging them up and taking a job as Royals vice president of baseball operations. The wondering was over for fans. It long since had ceased for Brett.

He said he'd known since the All-Star break. The one thing that could drive him away had happened. The man who'd played baseball with unsurpassed intensity simply had lost interest.

"The game beat me," he said. "It beats everybody. It took 26 years to beat Nolan Ryan, but it did. Now it's beaten me."

Winning didn't juice him the way it once did and losing didn't hurt as much. If *that* can happen to No. 5, you know it can happen to anyone. You know it is time to get out.

"Something was missing," he said. "It's like if you ride the same roller coaster 162 times a year for 20 years, you may want to try another ride. Space Mountain maybe. Mr. Toad's Wild Ride. You don't want to keep going down the Matterhorn bobsled."

Quirk said Brett was able to disguise such feelings to an extent that amazed him.

"He's always had the ability to block things out, with a level of concentration far beyond other players," Quirk said. "He could be saying, 'Jamie, I've had it,' one minute, then put it all out of his mind for three hours in a game.

"He never took it onto the field. Ever."

That's the quality Ken Brett liked best about his baby brother. "I am proudest that he played the game right," he said. "He ran hard, he played hard, and he played hurt. You just don't see that anymore."

Added Quirk, "He never gave an at-bat away. If he was four for four, he wanted five for five."

There just weren't enough four-for shells left in Brett's guns. And that bugged him. He might have had 17 homers and a team-leading 68 RBIs at the time of his announcement, but what he couldn't do ate away, way down deep.

"Guys depended on me in the clutch. I didn't do it. I had to admit I'm not the player I was anymore," he said.

Nothing could shake that.

"The other night in Oakland," Quirk recalled, "he hits the opposite-field homer — nobody hits opposite-field homers in Oakland. He got back to the dugout and I said, 'So I guess you're not going to retire now, huh?'

"He just said, 'Nope. I'm retiring.'"

Ken Brett understands completely: "He's hitting .270, but so what? To George, .270 is like .230. I got tired of picking up the paper and seeing him hitting .270. Him too. That's just not him."

What Brett is now is a suit-and-tie guy. Sort of. Looking at his navy blazer and khaki trousers, he deadpanned, "My first job is to get them to relax around here."

He joked about getting General Manager Herk Robinson to wear jeans. Humor seemed to help him ease into the idea of his new job.

"Now, instead of doing wind sprints in spring training, I'll be one of those guys eating tuna sandwiches in the coaches' offices," he said. "I always liked the idea of that."

Asked whether the new duties had enough teeth in them, he said, "Maybe I'm wrong, but I feel I have more to offer than sitting up there getting in people's way."

Same here. I think Brett will make an outstanding front-office guy. There always has been more to him than the I'm-just-a-ballplayer mentality he liked to project.

But the main thing he takes with him is the dead certainty he did the right thing. And he had, because at age 40, Peter Pan finally had the diamond dust and the kid beaten out of him.

"The game became a job. It wasn't a game anymore," Brett said.

Somehow, even as a daddy, watching him cuddle baby Jackson in his arms, it's hard to imagine George Brett without one foot still in never-never land. Yet he is forever changed now.

Now to see what the adult George Brett, off the base lines, sweating out real life in the slow lane, looks like.

Somehow, I think we're going to like him, too.

Throughout his career, George Brett always played with the fire, intensity, and pure joy of competition that have characterized the best ballplayers of the past 125 years.

EPILOGUE

THE LAST WORD

In his gracious and moving acceptance speech upon induction to the Hall of Fame in 1993, Reggie Jackson showed that keeping the game healthy for generations to come is both an honor and a responsibility.

I'll continue to be reminded that while I'm being honored by the Hall and all my loved ones who are here, and while this is my day, I'm just a link in the chain that makes the whole wheel go round and so too are today's players and those in the baseball community. So whether you're the "Babe," "Stan the Man," "Say Hey," or "Mr. October," you're just part of a long tradition of baseball and the game is owed our respect and gratitude. We all borrow from it, exploit it, cling to it and need it. The House that Ruth Built still stands, but the Babe's not there anymore. Henry's record still stands, but he's not even on the field anymore. "Mr. October" still surfaces in the fall, but he's not there in the summer. But for some unexplained reason the game still gives to us all. Whether we think we owe, take or borrow, baseball is a machine that requires each one of us to polish his part. And whether we're currently in or out of the game, we each need to remember that even if the wheel seems to wobble it still rolls on with or without us. We owe it to the fans and players coming along to keep it rolling because we're just caretakers for a short time. So if your name is Peter O'Malley, George Steinbrenner or Ted Turner, or whether your name is Kirby, Roger, Barry or Cal, realize you're just a part—just a link in the chain in the big scheme of things. Remember along the way that something we can all learn from these guys behind me is the need to humanize the game. I still feel energy when I see a player in the bigs who's in awe of Williams, Mantle, the "Big D," Koufax or Marichal or Clemente. Not because of a willingness to acknowledge the greatness of these giants, but because I know that the player of today needs to understand that his display of respect is needed for the game to endure. If the game is lost to the economics that drive it, we'll lose the humanity that is uniquely the game. We all must feel it and live it in our own way and be mindful of its vulnerability to abuse. From the millions to the billions that this game has come to represent, we all take from this cherished game. Stop and remember Buck O'Neil and "The Scooter" and all the people who played for the love of the game.

You may be worth what you get, but say thanks and remember the people who paved the way for you.

Some who paved the way: An informal A.L. all-star team, 1911. Front row (left to right): Germany Schaefer, Tris Speaker, Sam Crawford, James McAleer, Ty Cobb (wearing a Cleveland uniform because his own had been lost in transit), Gabby Street, Paddy Livingston. Back row: Bobby Wallace, Frank Baker, Joe Wood, Walter Johnson, Hal Chase, Clyde Milan, Russell Ford, Eddie Collins.

"BATTERIN' BABE"
"LOOK AT HIM NOW"
THE HOME RUN SONG HIT OF THE SEASON

Dedicated
TO
OUR OWN
"BABE RUTH"

WORDS
JACK O'BRIEN
MUSIC
BILLY TIMMINS

Sincerely yours
Babe Ruth

C. INTERNATIONAL

Published by
COLONIAL MUSIC PUBLISHING Co.
220 TREMONT ST. BOSTON-MASS.

TEXT CREDITS

PICTURE
CREDITS

INDEX

*Opposite: What the well-dressed
fan wore, Boston vs. Cleveland,
1903.*

289

Opposite: Mike "King" Kelly, devil-may-care star of major league baseball's early years.

The extraordinary Hack Wilson: "That short, fat, marvellous little player certainly can both hit and play the center field," remarked M. G. Bonner in The Big Baseball Book for Boys (1931) of the man who drove in 190 runs in 1930.

Overleaf: Frank Robinson (sliding) led both the Cincinnati Reds and Baltimore Orioles to the World Series during his twenty-one-year career.

Second overleaf: The Chicago Cubs' nonpareil second baseman, Ryne Sandberg.

Third overleaf: In a cloud of dirt, the play is over almost as soon as it begins, but—like countless others before and after—it remains in our memory.

Fourth overleaf: One pattern in baseball's ever-shifting kaleidoscope.